T&T CLARK STUDY GUIDES TO

THE ACTS OF THE APOSTLES

Series Editor
Tat-siong Benny Liew, College of the Holy Cross, USA

Other titles in the series include:

1&2 Thessalonians: An Introduction and Study Guide
1 Peter: An Introduction and Study Guide
2 Corinthians: An Introduction and Study Guide
Colossians: An Introduction and Study Guide
Ephesians: An Introduction and Study Guide
Galatians: An Introduction and Study Guide
James: An Introduction and Study Guide
John: An Introduction and Study Guide
Luke: An Introduction and Study Guide
Mark: An Introduction and Study Guide
Matthew: An Introduction and Study Guide
Philemon: An Introduction and Study Guide
Philippians: An Introduction and Study Guide
Romans: An Introduction and Study Guide
The Letters of Jude and Second Peter: An Introduction and Study Guide

T&T Clark Study Guides to the Old Testament:

1 & 2 Samuel: An Introduction and Study Guide
1 & 2 Kings: An Introduction and Study Guide
Ecclesiastes: An Introduction and Study Guide
Exodus: An Introduction and Study Guide
Ezra-Nehemiah: An Introduction and Study Guide
Hebrews: An Introduction and Study Guide
Leviticus: An Introduction and Study Guide
Jeremiah: An Introduction and Study Guide
Job: An Introduction and Study Guide
Joshua: An Introduction and Study Guide
Psalms: An Introduction and Study Guide
Song of Songs: An Introduction and Study Guide
Numbers: An Introduction and Study Guide

THE ACTS OF THE APOSTLES

An Introduction and Study Guide
Taming the Tongues of Fire

By
Shelly Matthews

Bloomsbury T&T Clark
An imprint of Bloomsbury Publishing Plc

B L O O M S B U R Y
LONDON · OXFORD · NEW YORK · NEW DELHI · SYDNEY

Bloomsbury T&T Clark
An imprint of Bloomsbury Publishing Plc

Imprint previously known as T&T Clark

50 Bedford Square	1385 Broadway
London	New York
WC1B 3DP	NY 10018
UK	USA

www.bloomsbury.com

**BLOOMSBURY, T&T CLARK and the Diana logo are trademarks of
Bloomsbury Publishing Plc**

First published 2013. This edition published 2017

British Library Cataloguing-in-Publication Data
A catalogue record for this book is available from the British Library.

ISBN: PB: 978-0-5676-7123-3
ePDF: 978-0-5676-7124-0
ePub: 978-0-5676-7125-7

Library of Congress Cataloging-in-Publication Data
A catalog record for this book is available from the Library of Congress.

Series: T&T Clark Study Guides to the New Testament, volume 5

Cover design: clareturner.co.uk

Typeset by Newgen Knowledge Works (P) Ltd., Chennai, India
Printed and bound in Great Britain

For my Parents,
Glen and Grace Matthews

Contents

You are reading this guide to the book of Acts at a time when biblical scholarship is in a period of great fluctuation. Were this guide written in the early to mid-twentieth century, readers would be introduced to Acts solely within the framework of the historical-critical method, the reigning method for studying the biblical text in academic settings during that era. Historical criticism, in distinction to traditional dogmatic approaches to the study of scripture, regards the biblical text as a text written by human authors, whose words can be critically analyzed in the same manner in which one might analyze any other humanly-authored text. Unlike dogmatic approaches concerned primarily with employing scripture as a time-less, ahistorical text with immediate relevance to contemporary spiritual questions, historical critics emphasize the importance of understanding the text within its ancient historical context.

The historical-critical paradigm is still a predominant approach to biblical studies in academic circles and this guide will introduce readers to many of the questions traditionally raised within this paradigm. These include questions of authorship and genre, the relationship of Acts to the Third Gospel, how to account for discrepancies between depictions of Paul in Acts and Paul's own autobiographical statements within his epistles and so forth. But in the early twenty-first century, the historical-critical paradigm is no longer the only approach on the academic table and, thus, readers need to be alerted to the pitfalls of this paradigm and offered a viable alternative for understanding what it means to read and interpret a biblical text in our present context.

Historical criticism, as it has traditionally been practiced (and here its traditional assumptions and tendencies are presented in their extreme forms for purposes of illustration), presumes a modern empiricist-scientific world-view. In this worldview, the text has one, and only one, fixed meaning. The task of the interpreter is to unearth this fixed meaning, as one might extract a kernel of grain from its husk, or unearth the bedrock lying beneath the sediment which has accrued upon it over long centuries. This one meaning could be discovered by anyone, anywhere (and, hence, is understood to be universally accessible), provided that the interpreter is equipped with proper philological training and, furthermore, provided that the interpreter assume a posture of neutrality and objectivity. The particular theological,

ethical and/or political effects of any meaning extracted or unearthed by
the historical critic would be understood to owe to the meaning residing
within the text itself. Thus the exegete could not be credited or faulted for
those theological, ethical and/or political effects, for the exegete is merely
engaged in the empirical discovery of what the text *really says.*

In the last decades of the twentieth century and into the twenty-first, this
modern scientific-empirical worldview has been called into question across
academic disciplines, including the discipline of biblical criticism. Those
leading the challenge in biblical scholarship have included feminists and
scholars from racial/ethnic minority groups within North America, along
with non-Western voices across the globe. In various ways, these scholars
have all argued that disembodied, disinterested readings of scripture are
impossible. For purposes of introduction, this challenge to the historical-
critical paradigm might be identified as three-pronged.

First, feminists and other theorists of domination have highlighted the
perspectival nature of all biblical interpretation, namely, that what one
sees in a text depends upon where one stands. Noting that the purportedly
objective universal reader of the historical-critical paradigm has, in actual-
ity, most often been an educated male of European ancestry whose readings have been contingent on his social circumstance, they foreground the
importance of social location (including identity markers such as gender,
race/ethnicity, class, nationality and sexual orientation) in the creation of
biblical meaning.

Second, they highlight the crucial role played by readers and reading
communities that are particularly located in time and space in activating
a text's meaning. In other words, they insist that texts have ideology or
agency only within (or as an effect of) the specific histories in which they
are read and that multiple readings of a text are possible. While this is a
principle widely held across humanities disciplines by those who challenge
modernist reading assumptions, biblical scholars are in a unique position
to illustrate it, owing to the fact that the Bible has been subject to thousands of readings over thousands of years. For example, even within the last
century of biblical criticism an enormous variety of scholarly perspectives
on the meaning of the infancy narratives in the Gospels of Matthew and
Luke has been generated—from Rudolf Bultmann's demythologized reading to Raymond Brown's *The Birth of the Messiah* to Richard Horsley's *The
Liberation of Christmas* to Jane Schaberg's *The Illegitimacy of Jesus.* The variety of readings generated expands even more vastly if one includes homilies
on the infancy narratives by ancient 'church fathers' (such as Origen or
Tertullian) or consults the spate of commentaries recently introduced by
non-hegemonic interpreters (including the *Queer Bible Commentary, True
to our Native Land: An African American New Testament Commentary, The
Global Bible Commentary* or *The Women's Bible Commentary*).

Third, they argue that biblical scholars cannot produce disinterested readings of texts, but that all readings have social and political consequence. Whether the issue is European colonial expansion in the modern world, antebellum struggles over slavery in the United States, on-going ecclesiastical debates concerning roles of women in the church or contemporary urgent debates concerning the ordination of sexual minorities and the issue of gay marriage, biblical texts are sites of struggle over power, norms and influence in religious communities and in the larger society as well.

In summary, beginning in the late twentieth and into the twenty-first century, biblical scholars attuned to theoretical currents in the fields of feminist, racial/ethnic minority, postcolonial and queer studies have posed three interrelated challenges to the reigning historical-critical paradigm. First, it has questioned the possibility of a universal reading, stressing the importance of social location in producing meaning; second, it has highlighted the role of the reader and reading communities in activating meaning in any text; third, it has highlighted the political nature of all biblical interpretation. In view of these challenges, these scholars argue that biblical exegetes should pay much more attention to the ethical consequences of their readings than they have up to this point. For instance, Elisabeth Schüssler Fiorenza has been in the forefront of scholars articulating the need for a shift from the historical-critical paradigm in biblical scholarship—along with a shift from the scriptural-theological paradigm dominant in fundamentalist and many traditional religious communities—to a rhetorical-ethical paradigm (e.g. Schüssler Fiorenza 1999). Understanding biblical scholarship as a rhetorical undertaking highlights the fact that biblical authors and readers, both ancient and modern, are not disinterestedly disclosing fixed meanings or Truth (with a capital T), but are rather engaged in struggles and contests over the construction of meaning. Understanding biblical interpretation as having ethical consequences is an acknowledgment that the Bible was written and is interpreted in patriarchal, racist and other contexts of domination. Interpreters can choose, in so far as their partial vision allows, either to resist or to collude with those dominant forces.

The author of this guide has been convinced of the need to embrace the rhetorical-ethical paradigm of biblical scholarship. Consequently, decisions about what to emphasize and what to overlook in this introductory guide (and decisions about what to include and what to omit are essential for any author who puts pen to paper, whether explicitly stated or not) are based in no small part on my understanding of which issues are of greatest consequence for those who work with biblical texts in faith communities and in other public forums in which biblical interpretation matters. However, the rhetorical-ethical and historical-critical paradigms need not be understood as mutually exclusive. The standard introductory questions raised in historical-critical schools receive primary focus in Chapters One and Two of this guide; they will inform the rest of the book as well. Chapter Three focuses on the question of Acts and Empire; this ongoing conversation concerning imperial force and its consequences for subjects of empire in antiquity is also relevant to modern interrogations of empire. Chapter Four is devoted to the question of Acts on Jews and Judaism, owing to my awareness that the problem of Christian anti-Judaism is complex and longstanding and that it stems in no small part from narrative depictions of non-believing Jews as murderous and vile in the Acts narrative. The question of Acts and the Jews taken up in Chapter Four also engages issues of empire, since Acts' rhetorical assertions concerning non-believing Jews can only be understood in terms of this broader political context. The passage chosen for an in-depth exegesis in the concluding chapter is the Pentecost pericope in Acts 2, because narrative details here—for example, the gathering of nations in Jerusalem, the tongues of flame, the multiple languages spoken, the democratizing force of the Spirit—along with possibilities for reading the passage against the grain make it a fruitful site for demonstrating the payoffs of the rhetorical-ethical paradigm.

Finally, it should be acknowledged that the dogmatic-theological paradigm has also influenced my own reading, if in a complicated and partial way. I was raised in a Protestant tradition (in a United Methodist church on the North Dakota prairie) and, eventually, became an ordained member of the clergy in that tradition. I embrace many of the ecclesial teachings of the church into which I was born and the social gospel strand of Methodism, to which I was introduced in those early years, helps to explain my interest in ethical aspects of biblical interpretation. I also emphatically repudiate other aspects of that ecclesial tradition, noting particularly that, in the summer of 2012 as this manuscript comes to completion, the majority of my own denominational representatives have chosen to stand on the side of oppression—and on the wrong side of history—in their recent decrees on the question of homosexuality. Because ecclesial bodies hold tremendous power, both for liberation and for oppression, and continue to exercise their power in both of these directions, a theological approach to scriptural interpretation must always be weighed within the rhetorical-historical-ethical paradigm for its liberating or oppressive potential.

An Introductory Word Concerning Terms and Definitions Used in the Guide

Authorship

Dogmatic Christian tradition ascribes authorship of both the Third Gospel and Acts to a man named Luke; this Luke is supposed to have been a companion to Paul, through whom Luke had eyewitness access to the spread of the Gospel. This guide ascribes, instead, to the judgment of historical criticism that these two texts, like the other canonical Gospels, were written anonymously and that the tradition of the named author, Luke, does not arise until late second-century battles over the definition of heresy required the attribution of these writings to named apostles and their closest associates. While acknowledging that the work is anonymous, I will, nevertheless, employ the name 'Luke' as a conventional means of designating the writer in question, though only in instances when it is clear that Luke designates the *author* of Luke–Acts. This guide will also make frequent use of the phrases, 'the author of Acts' and 'the Third Gospel' in order to avoid confusion as to whether, in any particular instance, 'Luke' designates the author (a person) or the Gospel (a text).

The guide also assumes the historical-critical principle that the writer who put Luke and Acts into final form did not create a text *de novo*, but worked from pre-existing written sources. While, technically, this means that the writer might better be designated as a redactor or editor rather than an author, I retain the word author in this guide. It is the word that best captures Luke's role in composing narrative as well as redacting traditions to which he had access. Readers should note that ancient authors, such as Luke, freely absorbed previously written works—sometimes verbatim, sometimes with modification—into their own writings without feeling the obligation to credit those sources. I use author, then, in this expanded sense, as one who puts a text into final form, but who is not bound by the conventions of originality that generally adhere to modern notions of authorship. (Again, technically here, one should say 'approximately final form' rather than final form in any absolute sense, as ancient texts, including biblical texts, were much more fluid than modern ones; they were subject to modifications, expansions and other types of editorial comment. The book of Acts, in particular, is known to have circulated in a 'maverick' version [with obvious and substantial editorial revision] in the Western tradition.)

A final note on authorship: when resorting to a gendered pronoun for this author, 'he' will be employed consistently. To be sure, feminist biblical scholars have made compelling cases that women also contributed to the composition of biblical narrative, whether through oral or written composition, and it is likely that even Luke builds on sources composed by women. Yet I adopt the male pronoun to designate this author, primarily because the ideal author is coded as male (consider the masculine particle used for self-reference in Lk. 1.3, *parēkoluthēkoti*). Furthermore, as will be demonstrated throughout the guide, the text of Acts has a particularly stark androcentric focus.

Christian/Jew

It is now widely held among biblical scholars that Christianity did not emerge as a separate religion, distinct from Judaism, already in the first century. The earliest followers of Jesus were all Jewish and even the first generation(s) of Gentile Jesus-followers understood themselves as part of 'Israel' in ways that did not require them to think of non-believing Jews as entirely and distinctly other. In some places and cases the lines between what would constitute Christianity, as opposed to Judaism, were hard to draw for centuries even beyond the first. Thus, it is common, at present, in biblical scholarship to avoid using the terms Christian and Christianity for Jesus believers of the first century. In support of a preference to avoid the term Christian in speaking of Jesus believers in the book of Acts, it might also be noted that the author of Acts himself does not fully embrace the term. He prefers instead the term 'believers', along with 'brothers' and 'followers of the Way'.

Because I date the book of Acts to the second rather than the first century (for reasons to be elaborated in a subsequent chapter), I am less reluctant to use the term 'Christian' for the social group the emergence of which Luke narrates. This designation for Jesus believers comes to be used in the early second century both by biblical authors and outsiders. The early second-century authors Tacitus, Suetonius and Pliny know of the name and Luke himself uses it in Acts twice [11.26 and 26.28]; the second-century New Testament text, 1 Peter, also knows the term [1 Pet. 4.16]). Though I agree that the break between Christians and Jews has not been achieved with any fullness by the time of Luke's writing, I also argue that Luke himself, especially in the book of Acts, is quite interested in asserting that a break is in the process of occurring between his social group and other Jews. Thus, the term Christian is occasionally employed in this guide to designate the social group at the center of Luke's focus. But more often, in acknowledgement of Luke's own avoidance of this term, I will employ 'Jesus believer' or 'Follower of the Way'.

Distinguishing Luke's followers of 'the Way' from other Jews in his narrative also requires translation decisions. Because *hoi Ioudaioi* is often used in Acts with a negative force (not unlike its employment in the Fourth Gospel), some have suggested that it should remain untranslated; others would stress the locative connotation and translate as 'Judeans'. In this guide, I have opted to retain the traditional option 'the Jews'. In order to signal that this is Luke's term employed in a particular historical context, rather than a blanket term for Jews in all times and places, I will set the term in quotation marks. Because Luke insists that leaders of his movement are also *Ioudaioi* (for reasons to be explored in subsequent chapters), I most often designate Jews outside of Luke's own social group as 'non-believing Jews'; that is, those who don't confess Jesus as messiah. This is not, of course, to suggest that Luke regarded Jews as having no beliefs whatsoever, but that, for Luke, the distinction between "true Jews" and "the Jews" hinged on the question of belief in Jesus.

Kyriarchy/kyriocentric

I adopt this neologism, coined by the feminist biblical scholar, Elisabeth Schüssler Fiorenza, as a more precise means of theorizing domination than the more widely used terms, patriarchy and androcentric. Patriarchy (literally 'rule of the fathers') and androcentrism (literally 'male centeredness') suggest a gendered, binary construction of systems of domination and oppression in which men rule over women. *Kyriarchy*, or rule of the master or lord, allows for a more complex understanding of systems of domination and oppression where gender intersects with other identity markers, including class and ethnicity.

Ekklēsia/Assembly

Though the Greek word *ekklēsia* is commonly translated into English as 'church', I will often retain the Greek spelling as a reminder that early Christians chose a term for their communal gatherings derived from the Greek *polis*, which signals the democratic assembly of full citizens of that city. I will also use 'assembly' in translating *ekklēsia* in order to evoke this notion of civic gathering. The English word church has come to connote an established institution in Western society, most often embodied within kyriarchal and androcentric frameworks. Terms such as *ekklēsia* and assembly, in contrast, evoke a more utopian notion of a society of equals engaged in political deliberation.

For Further Reading

Bailey, Randall C., Tat-siong Benny Liew and Fernando F. Segovia (eds.)
2009 *They Were All Together in One Place? Toward Minority Biblical Criticism* (Atlanta, GA: Society of Biblical Literature).
Blount, Brian K. (ed.)
2007 *True to Our Native Land: An African American New Testament Commentary* (Minneapolis, MN: Fortress Press).
Guest, Deryn, Robert Goss, Mona West and Thomas Bohache (eds.)
2006 *The Queer Bible Commentary* (London: SCM Press).
Martin, Dale
2006 'Introduction: The Myth of Textual Agency', in *Sex and the Single Savior* (Louisville, KY: Westminster John Knox Press), pp. 1-16.

Newsom, Carol and Sharon Ringe (eds.)
1998   *The Women's Bible Commentary* (Louisville, KY: Westminster John Knox Press, expanded edn).
Patte, Daniel (ed.)
2004   *The Global Bible Commentary* (Nashville, TN: Abingdon).
Schüssler Fiorenza, Elisabeth
1999   *Rhetoric and Ethic: The Politics of Biblical Studies* (Minneapolis, MN: Fortress Press).
Segovia, Fernando and Mary Ann Tolbert (eds.)
1995   *Reading from This Place* (2 vols.; Minneapolis, MN: Fortress Press).
Wimbush, Vincent
2011   'Interpreters—Enslaving/Enslaved/Runagate', *JBL* 130, pp. 5-24.

1

Traditional Questions in Acts Scholarship

This first chapter takes up many of the questions concerning the book of Acts that scholars have raised since the beginning of modern biblical criticism. Thus, these questions fall largely under the historical-critical paradigm, though it should be noted that the rhetorical-ethical framework adopted for the book as a whole shapes even this traditional overview. In keeping with the understanding that biblical texts are rhetorical arguments, the chapter devotes a good amount of time to situating Acts as a text with a particular point of view, written for the purposes of persuasion. It also pays attention to how that perspective is presented in terms of gender, class and politics, noting, for instance, that the book of Acts is addressed to an elite patron, the most excellent Theophilus, and strives to present an account of the Jesus movement that offers Theophilus security and reassurance. Starting already in this chapter, we will gesture to points at which Luke's narrative appears to mask or suppress 'less orderly' aspects of the movement. These points will be returned to repeatedly in the book as places where other early Christian voices aside from Luke's own might be retrieved. We turn now to our review of introductory questions.

Luke–Acts or Luke and Acts? The Relationship between These Two Volumes

The Gospel of Luke and the book of Acts do not stand side by side in the New Testament as it is canonized. Indeed, there are no existing ancient codices in which the two works stand in sequence; in manuscripts of the New Testament, where they are both present, they are always separated by the Gospel of John. Despite the distance that separates them in the canon, the majority of biblical scholars concur that these two volumes share a common author. The question is whether these two volumes were originally intended by their author to be read as one continuous work (those advocating in favor of this position generally use the hyphenated title: Luke–Acts) or whether Acts constitutes a separate writing which the author envisioned as standing independently of the Gospel. Readers of an introductory guide such as this need not fall decisively on either side of this question, but it will be useful to begin by rehearsing both the key distinctions between the two volumes and their obvious similarities.

How These Two Volumes Differ

The Third Gospel is focused on the life, death and resurrection of Jesus. It situates that life within the geographical terrain of Galilee and Judea, which Jesus traverses to meet his fated death and ultimate triumph in the city of Jerusalem. In terms of its genre, this Gospel is related to the three other canonical Gospels, and especially to Mark, from which it draws its narrative frame, and to Matthew, with which it shares the Markan framing along with a large body of sayings attributed to Jesus. Acts, in contrast, is the story of the mission and expansion of the post-Easter assembly (*ekklēsia*), as well as how that expansion is guided by the Holy Spirit and shaped by its leaders. In the first twelve chapters, this leadership is exercised by the Jerusalem apostles (with Peter as their primary spokesperson) and by James, the brother of Jesus. Saul/Paul becomes the chief protagonist of the book from Acts 13 onward; after receiving authorization from Peter and James and the Jerusalem apostles and elders, Paul carries out his Gentile mission from Acts 15 to the end of the story. Like the Third Gospel, Acts is ordered as a sort of travelogue, but the geographical scope expands significantly. While travel in the Third Gospel is limited to Galilee, Samaria and Judea, much larger swaths of the ancient Mediterranean world are traversed by Paul and the apostles and even larger swaths of territory are invoked in Acts. Consider the geographic diversity of those who gather on the day of Pentecost (Parthians, Elamites, Cappadocians, Egyptians, *et al.*; see 2.5-11), the wide-ranging list of native homes of those involved in the stoning of Stephen (Cyrenians, Alexandrians, Cilicians and Asians; 6.9), or the story of the Ethiopian chamberlain traveling homeward from Jerusalem and receiving a baptism along the way (8.26-40). The expansion of the Way involves circuitous travel—three journeys beginning from the eastern Mediterranean toward the Aegean Sea and then back to Jerusalem (Acts12–21). Yet the narrative also has an overarching linear, westward thrust: the movement that begins in Jerusalem, the capital city of the Jews, ends in the city of Rome, the greatest city of the great (Gentile) empire.

As one of four canonical Gospels, the Third Gospel must necessarily participate in a rehearsal of the story of Jesus that contains cacophony and multiplicity. This cacophony and multiplicity result in notable discrepancies among the Gospels, including how Jesus is said to die both before and after eating a Passover meal (cf. John and Mark on the timing of Jesus' death in relation to the Passover meal) or how Jesus is said to teach only in parables according to Mark (Mk. 4.33-34), but is never acknowledged as a teacher of parables in John. Just to give one more example, Mark and Matthew depict Jesus as angst-ridden in the garden of Gethsemane, where he rolls on the ground in agony at the prospect of his death, while both Luke and

John depict Jesus as meeting his death fully composed and in a posture of self-mastery.

Unlike the Third Gospel, which can be set alongside the other three Gospels for the sake of comparison and contrast, Acts is unique among New Testament books in terms of its content and literary genre. It is the only canonical narrative of events taking place among the believers after the resurrection and ascension of Jesus. Acts' singularity—and the accompanying question of what diverse expressions of belief in Jesus have been lost through the canonization of only one such narrative—will be a point of continued reflection throughout this guide.

How These Two Volumes are Related

While we may speak of these two volumes as bearing distinctive generic traits and themes, it is, nevertheless, the case that they are also related. One key indication of their relationship is the large number of thematic parallels between them. In Acts, Peter and Paul are depicted as preaching the same message and performing the same sorts of miracles and exorcisms that Jesus had in the Third Gospel (on preaching the kingdom of God, cf. Lk. 4.43, Acts 19.8; 28.31; for healings and other miracles, compare Lk. 6.18-19; 13.13; 18.42 with Acts 3.7; 5.12, 15-16; 8.13; 19.11; for a parallel exorcism, compare Lk. 8.26-39 and Acts 16.16-18). The fate of Stephen (Acts 6–8.1), as well as those of Peter and Paul, is clearly patterned on the fate of Jesus in the Third Gospel. All are sent by God to deliver prophetic oracles, all are rejected by Israel, all suffer persecution in Jerusalem. The charge against Jesus in Luke, that he has 'corrupted the Jewish people and prevented others from paying taxes to Caesar' (Lk. 23.2), is echoed in the charge against Paul that he instigates rebellion among the people (Acts 24.5; cf. 16.21; 17.7). A case for a tight linkage of Luke and Acts can be made through consideration of how this author treats the elements of the passion narrative it borrows from Mark. The author knows of the charge that Jesus intends to destroy the temple (Mk 14.58); rather than including it in his description of Jesus' passion, he reserves the charge to be leveled against Stephen instead (Acts 6.14). This is also true of (1) the charge of blasphemy, which is directed in Mk 14.64 against Jesus; it is not included in the trial of Jesus in the Gospel of Luke, but then crops up in the book of Acts as an accusation against Stephen in 6.11; and (2) the characterization of the accusers as false witnesses, which is present in Mk 14.56-57 and in Acts 6.13, but absent from the Third Gospel. While in many instances the author of the Third Gospel shapes his account of Jesus' passion according to the text of Mark that stands before him, the fact that he has reserved elements of Mark's story for his second volume suggests that he has both volumes in mind, even as he writes the first.

One also finds evidence of a relationship between the two volumes at their seams. Both the ending of Luke (24.36-53) and the beginning of Acts (1.3-12) cover the same themes: the presence of the resurrected Jesus among the apostles; the promise of the coming of the Holy Spirit and the exhortation to the eleven to remain in Jerusalem until the Spirit's arrival; Jesus' ascent into the heavens. The ending of Acts also echoes themes introduced in the early chapters of Luke. Paul's 'preaching of the kingdom of God' in the final verse of Acts (28.31) reverberates back to the preaching of the apostles, as well as to that of John the Baptist and Jesus himself (Lk. 4.18; 8.2; 9.2). Paul's final speech in Acts, a quotation from the prophet Isaiah employed to explain Jewish rejection of the gospel and its more favorable reception among the Gentiles (28.26-28), parallels Simeon's prophecy in the Temple in the Third Gospel concerning this 'light to the Gentiles' which is destined for the 'falling ... of many in Israel' (2.29-35). Another link with great significance is the preface of Luke (1.1-4), which is referred to in the preface of Acts, which begins at Acts 1.1, but contains no clear resolution (the point at which the preface of Acts ends is debated). The Third Gospel opens with a first person address to the 'most excellent Theophilus' and lays out a rationale and a plan for the composition that will follow. Acts hooks back to that preface, if briefly, in 1.1, before plunging into its narrative account: "In the first book, Theophilus, I wrote about all that Jesus did and taught from the beginning" (NRSV). The significance of the Lukan preface and what it might mean for the reading of Acts requires further consideration.

The Lukan Preface

Three aspects of the preface of the Third Gospel are noted here as useful for understanding the overarching rhetorical aims of Acts. First, the work is addressed to a patron, the 'most excellent Theophilus', who is invoked by name again in Acts 1.1. It is possible that these two works were actually written for a historical person bearing such a name. Alternatively, it is also possible that Theo-philus (in Greek, literally, 'God-lover') is merely one instance of this author's penchant for sprinkling his narrative with symbolic names, with the name here serving as an invitation to any pious and literate person seeking truth to take up the work and read. In ancient literary circles, addressing a work to a specific patron was not meant to limit its circulation to a narrow audience; the work would still have been offered for a larger educated public so inclined to read it (in this case, beyond Theophilus and his circle). Therefore, to argue whether Theophilus is a historical rather than fictitious patron is merely to argue over a very thin difference: either the book is addressed to any lover of God (none of whose names we know) or it is addressed to any lover of God (including one historical patron named

Theophilus, about whom little else can be said). Yet, historical or not, the attribution to Theophilus of the phrase 'most excellent' provides a significant clue concerning the ideal reader crafted by this author.

The superlative address, 'most excellent', is a marker of high-status, commonly signaling a man with governmental responsibilities (compare the remaining instances of the usage in Acts at 23.26; 24.3; 26.25). The title was once used as a piece of supporting evidence for the theory that Acts was written to a high-ranking Roman official in an attempt to persuade him that Christianity was politically innocuous. This specific theory, positing a Roman officer outside of the movement as the primary recipient of Acts, is no longer pervasive; it was cut down famously by C.K. Barrett in his dry assessment: 'No Roman official would ever have filtered out so much of what to him would be theological and ecclesiastical rubbish in order to reach so tiny a grain of relevant apology ...' (Barrett 1961: 63). The probable first readers of this work would have been among the educated classes, something that might be deduced from the fact that Luke employs conventions in his work that would have appealed to those participating in a literary culture. But they were also probably not from the highest ranking of the educated classes, given what is generally known of the social status of Christians in the early second century. Further, it is also likely that the readers were insiders of the movement, rather than outsiders, who, like the ideal reader Theophilus, were looking for further reassurance concerning the things to which they had already assented. From Lk. 1.4 ('that you may know the truth concerning the things *about which you have been instructed* [*katēcheō*]'), we may deduce that Theophilus is presumed to come to the writings of Luke and Acts with some knowledge of the movement already in hand.

From such a position, the author of the Third Gospel and Acts and their readers were seeking legitimation for their movement, reassurance that they had joined an association that was respectable and grounded in historical truth; one that should not put them in harm's way were they to come to the attention of governing authorities. To know from the start that Acts was written for the 'most excellent Theophilus' would provide the sort of reassurance they sought.

Acts bears much evidence that it is written with the perspective of a high status patron in mind, whether real or imaginary. To say this another way, Acts is written to affirm an elite sensibility of what a stable and legitimate social grouping in the ancient Roman world should look like: it is led by men (and masculine gender is key here), who speak publicly with boldness (*parrēsia*), who resolve internal discord through careful deliberation, who do not engage in civic unrest (in spite of false charges to the contrary) and who practice a long-established form of piety, based on the teachings of an ancient lawgiver.

A second key feature of the Lukan preface, which also serves to illuminate the nature of Acts, is the indication that the author is writing at some
distance from the earliest events concerning the movement about which he
narrates. As Luke sits down to pen the first volume, he acknowledges the
existence of other written narratives: 'Many have undertaken to set down
an orderly account of the events that have been fulfilled among us', Lk. 1.1.
Both he, and those whose written reports he knows, are removed in time
from those who first handed down stories of the events from which Luke
now attempts to craft an orderly account: 'just as they were delivered to us
by those who from the beginning were eyewitnesses and ministers of the word',
Lk. 1.2. While some scholars have suggested that Luke claims eyewitness
status for himself in the preface, this is a somewhat difficult position to
defend in view of the fact that at 1.2 Luke puts himself among those to
whom the eyewitnesses passed the tradition.

In the interpretive tradition of the 'Church Fathers', Luke's concession
that he is not among the eyewitnesses to those things that occurred from the
beginning is thought to apply only to the Gospel of Luke and not to the book
of Acts. This ancient traditional perspective held that, in writing the second
volume, a historical person named Luke, as Paul's companion, was privileged to be recording events for which he did, indeed, possess an eyewitness
perspective. The 'proof' for this eyewitness standing comes from the 'we'
passages contained in Acts, where there is a sudden shift in narration from
the third person to the first person plural. Clustered around the sea-voyages,
these passages read as if they come from a traveler's diary (see 16.10-17;
20.5–21.18; 27.1–28.16). As the ancient church historian Eusebius puts it,
in contrast to the Third Gospel, 'The Acts of the Apostles ... he composed
no longer on the evidence of hearing but of his own eyes' (*Hist. eccl.* 3.4.6).

While it may be conceded that through the so-called we-passages the
author wishes to suggest that he was Paul's traveling companion, most Acts
scholars regard that claim as a literary fiction and consider *both* volumes to
be governed by a retrospective point of view. I will elaborate the argument
that Acts, like the Third Gospel, is written at a considerable distance from
the events it narrates when I discuss the date of Acts' composition (see
below). Here I make only the general observation that the coherence of the
Acts narrative belies the idea that the author writes *in medias res*. As anyone
who recognizes the difference between a historian writing at a quiet desk
and a journalist composing dispatches from the front lines will concede, it
is hard to gain a handle on the significance of events immediately as they
unfold. The author of Acts has a much fuller view of events than a journalist would; this is indicated, for example, in the way events unfold precisely
as they should, by the neat parallels drawn between actions of each of the
protagonists or by the confident assertion that the unfolding events fulfill

the scriptures in their entirety. Such tightly woven patterns of coherence require an author who can consider past events from some remove.

Third and certainly related to points one and two, the author proposes to write an 'orderly' account so that his reader might know the truth (or, the surety or security [*asphaleia*]) about the things he has been taught. Truth or security—*asphaleia*—is the final word of the long Greek sentence which constitutes the Lukan preface and, as such, bears a special emphasis. The suggestion that the author knows of other accounts, but that, through his careful and orderly compilation, he will provide security to Theophilus, carries an implicit criticism of those other accounts; those previous accounts are presumed by Luke to be less orderly, less secure and, hence, in need of correction. Because one of the sources Luke used for his Gospel is readily available in the Gospel of Mark, we can see several instances in which Luke did, indeed, modify a written source to make his own account more orderly and, thus, more suitable to the ideal reader at whom he aims. (As one of many examples of how Luke edits a source to make it more palatable to a literary audience, note how the Gospel of Luke, in contrast to the Gospel of Mark, downplays Jesus' emotional agony, both in the garden of Gethsemane [cf. Mk 14.32-42; Lk. 22.39-46] and as he dies on the cross [cf. Mk 15.33-37; Lk. 23.27-46], so that Jesus' death conforms to the noble deaths of Greek philosophers that would have been familiar to his literate audience.)

As noted above, while we have only one canonical narrative of the things that happened among the earliest Jesus believers after Jesus' resurrection, it is likely that there was more cacophony and multiplicity among Jesus believers concerning the significance of this time than this one narrative suggests. In addition to the Markan account of the life and death of Jesus, upon which Luke feels compelled to improve, one might point to other sources, including non-canonical sources, suggesting theological insights and diverse perspectives which Luke wishes to mute. Theophilus might have had no patience for unruly speaking in tongues in Corinth or female teachers and spokespersons for the movement like Mary Magdalene. For the purposes of providing a narrative that was orderly and secure, Luke has engaged in a process of 'cleaning up' the story, including a winnowing out of details that might subvert such order.

These three aspects of the Lukan preface—(1) that it is addressed to the most excellent Theophilus; (2) that it is written as a retrospective, after the passing of a considerable amount of time; and (3) that it promises an orderly account in order to provide surety—will serve as points of reflection throughout this guide to Acts. But before we turn to these larger explorations, other introductory matters must be addressed, including the question of the relationship of this text to the historical events it purports to narrate.

Acts and the Question of Genre

It is often argued that for a text to be interpreted properly, its precise generic classification must first be ascertained. If this were true, the usefulness of this introductory guide would be seriously curtailed, since Acts does not fit neatly into an ancient generic classification. In recent scholarship, Acts (and sometimes Luke–Acts, if and when read together) has been categorized as a species of epic, modeled ambitiously upon Virgil's *Aeneid* (and, thus, also upon Homer, Virgil's model; see Bonz 2000); as a 'succession narrative appended to a biography' modeled on a pattern found in accounts of the lives of certain philosophers in the Greek author, Diogenes Laertius (see Talbert 1974); and as a historical narrative. Among those who argue for Acts as history, further suggestions or subdivisions are made to view its genre in terms of political historiography (Balch 1989), general history (Aune 1987), monograph (Conzelmann 1987), apologetic historiography (Sterling 1992; Penner 2004) and institutional historiography (Cancik 1997). It has also been proposed that the text bears many resemblances to the ancient novel (Pervo 1987; Smith 1995). Acts contains similarities with literature in each of these genres, but in every case dissimilarities also abound. Thus, no scholarly consensus has been reached.

Fortunately, we do not have to pin down the question of genre with precision in order to progress toward a deeper understanding of the text. A few general observations about the kind of literature before us should suffice here. First, at the most general level, it can be readily acknowledged that Acts does refer to historical events: the death of Jesus of Nazareth and the proclamation of his resurrection, the missionary activity of Paul and the emergence of *assemblies* in major cities along the Aegean coastline can be safely considered as historical occurrences. Therefore, the work is to be distinguished from 'pure' fiction, if such fiction is understood to comprise a genre in which historical referentiality is suspended altogether (for this understanding of fiction, see Konstan 1998). We can say further that, while Acts speaks of historical events, it is not ancient Greek historiography in the strict sense; that is, it is not history in the manner of a Thucydides or a Polybius, as neither the subject matter nor the prose style conforms to this ancient genre. These loftiest of ancient Greek historians focused their eyes on war and great men of war; they also wrote in a refined style of Greek that the author of Acts might gesture toward, but cannot sustain.

Acts can be placed somewhere between the poles of pure fiction and classic Greek historiography. It also shares commonalities with biblical history. As is the case with the narrative books of the Septuagint, Luke presumes that history is the unfolding of a divine plan for the salvation of God's chosen people and that great men, of humble origins, are called by God to be instruments in the execution of that plan. That Luke has a Septuagintal model in mind for his prose is also evident by the frequent citations of the Septuagint in his narrative.

In short, the text is some kind of historical narrative, with a biblical view of divine agency. But in order to appreciate fully what kind of 'historical' narrative Acts is, it needs to be underscored that the expressed aim of this ancient author is to provide surety or truth to his readers. Unlike modern understandings of what 'truth telling' should entail, an author's ability to establish such surety in the ancient world was not a matter of assuming the posture of neutrality or objectivity. Furthermore, establishing surety did not necessarily involve scrupulous research into the question of 'what really happened'. Ancient historians, rather, assumed the rhetorical task of persuasion. For an introductory reader of ancient historical narratives, and especially of historical narratives contained in the Bible, this aspect of such narratives might prove to be most alien and most discombobulating. Therefore, let us turn to a fuller consideration of the way that persuasive rhetoric and the ancient narration of historical events are intertwined.

Acts among Ancient Historical Narratives

When a twenty-first century reader, steeped in assumptions concerning the writing of modern history, picks up a text claiming to work from the testimony of eyewitnesses and disclosing the author's intention to provide a true account, she might expect to be engaging with an author whose primary concern is to relate, with as much precision and neutrality as possible, historical events 'as they really happened'. If, in contrast, she has had exposure to poststructuralist ideas (or what one might loosely call 'postmodern' ideas) about the relationship of events to narratives concerning those events, she knows that any narrative history involves choices about which events to highlight and precisely which words to use in the process of narration. She knows that there is not one and only one way in which a historical event might be translated into language and, further, that choices about how to emplot a narrative vary according to the present concerns, perspectives and biases of the author. She knows, in short, that there is no way to capture an event in language without making choices about what to say and what to leave out; there is, thus, neither a perfectly accurate nor a neutral way to tell a story about what 'really' happened in the past.

A reader with this latter perspective may have an easier time thinking about the relationship of Acts to historical events among early Christians because ancient authors were also critically and self-consciously aware that choices about how to write history needed to be made and that these choices shaped and molded their present and influenced their own standing within it. But either reader, whether the one who identifies more with modern or postmodern schools of history, would still benefit from further consideration of how the assumptions of ancient writers differ from those in the modern and postmodern age.

Imitation, Not Innovation

One key difference between our age and theirs is that the world in which the author of Acts lived was one that valued imitation and spurned innovation. The school system of the ancient world was built around the principle of imitating successful precursors. Students engaged in literary education in the Greco-Roman world, particularly those in advanced composition, would have been familiar with literature regarded as worthy of imitation. (These would include the writings of Homer, Euripides and Plato; for Luke himself— and unlike Hellenistic authors outside of Jewish circles—the Septuagint was also undoubtedly included within the category of worthy predecessors.) Through such an educational system, students engaged in writing exercises were schooled to shape their stories according to familiar models from their cultural repertoire. In imitating a model, one could include matters not only of word choice, but also of literary style, themes and characterization.

This impulse toward the imitation of earlier models is evident throughout the book of Acts and often provides considerably more explanatory value for interpreting a scene from Acts than the more modern assessment, 'Luke must have written his account in that way because that is the way that it really happened.' In support of this observation, consider the following examples:

1. *Socrates Redux.* In Acts 17, Paul travels to Athens, which was famous in the ancient world as the epicenter of Greek culture and artistry; Athens was infamous also for its decision to sentence Socrates, the greatest of all Greek philosophers, to death. Paul, after an obligatory stop in the synagogue, engages with crowds in the marketplace, like Socrates before him (17.17). He is, however, soon apprehended and brought before the council of the Areopagus where he is called to answer charges that he appears to be promoting 'foreign gods' (*xenōn daimoniōn*, 17.18). The accusation of promoting foreign gods among the youth in Athens was famously hung around the neck of Socrates by a fourth-century Athenian jury. No ancient audience could miss the fact that Luke is here crafting a scene for Paul on the model of this renowned philosopher.

2. *The Gods in Disguise.* Ovid's *Metamorphosis* preserves a Phrygian tradition that Jupiter and Mercury (Roman gods corresponding to the

Greek Zeus and Hermes) once disguised themselves as mortals and descended into the Phrygian hillside to test the hospitality of various inhabitants of the land (*Metamorphoses* 8.610-700). Acts 14.8-18 narrates the journey of Paul and Barnabas to Lystra, a city—in the region of Phrygia—where, after the healing of a lame man, they themselves are taken to be Zeus and Hermes: 'When the crowds saw what Paul had done, they shouted in the Lycaonian language, "The gods have come down to us in human form!"' (14.11). This is a scene that is widely recognized as an indication that the author of Acts made use of a culturally situated story, adapting it to provide local color to the story of Paul's missionary travels.

3. *Just like Dionysos*. The pattern of an unjustly persecuted but, ultimately, vindicated missionary of a foreign god was widely known in the ancient Greco-Roman world, owing to the popularity of the Dionysos cult and, particularly, to the popularity of the Dionysos myth, as it is preserved by the Greek playwright Euripides in the *Bacchae*. In broad strokes, the story line of the *Bacchae* runs as follows: the missionary of the foreign cult arrives in town, makes initial converts among the women of the city, meets resistance from the establishment and is unjustly imprisoned. Though he first undergoes persecution, he is, ultimately, vindicated through a miraculous prison escape. Many scholars have recognized Acts' imitation of this pattern in Paul's journey to Philippi (16.11-40). Arriving from the East, Paul's first encounter with a group of Philippians takes place at a synagogue populated by women and outside the city gates (that the gathering at the synagogue appears to be composed only of women sounds particularly odd, unless one recognizes the Dionysian pattern of approaching the women first). He then encounters opposition from officials who arrest him. Miraculously, an earthquake comes in the middle of the night, shaking the foundations of the prison and loosening the chains of the prisoners, including those of Paul and Silas. The fact that Paul and Silas are said to sing hymns in prison (16.25) serves as another literary allusion to the *Bacchae* (and, neatly folded into it, lies another allusion to Socratic endurance of persecution) because traditions developed that the *Bacchae* encouraged each other through song while in chains, as Socrates did before them. Consider this epigram preserved in the writings of the philosopher, Epictetus: 'And then we shall be emulating Socrates, when we are able to write paeans in prison' [Epictetus 2.6.26]).

These are but three among dozens of instances in Acts where it is clear that the author crafts his narrative in imitation of early models. Another impulse guiding the Acts narrative, not unrelated to this impulse toward imitation, is the ancient rhetorical principle of suitability that comes into play for authors writing historical narrative.

Telling the Story as It Should Have Happened

As odd as it may sound to a historian schooled in modern principles of writing historical narrative, the ancient historian was driven far more by the principle of 'fittingness'—what a character should say, or how a situation should unfold—than by any principle of 'accuracy'. Ancient authors were not bound by the modern notion that a historian is obligated to report only what really happened. We might connect this ancient understanding of history to the notions of Aristotle, the fourth-century Athenian philosopher.

Aristotle had classified poetry as more elevated than history, reasoning that poetry taught timeless truths rather than mere particulars (*Poetics* 9). Historians, responding to Aristotle's criticism, sought to elevate their own craft to the height of the poets by shaping their narratives of the past with an eye to the ways such narratives, like poetry, could also elicit timeless truths for the future. Thus, all subsequent histories in the ancient Greek and Roman world—even those prefaced by claims to eyewitness, thorough research and truth-telling—involved a complex weaving together of historical events, invented stories and persuasive artifice. The Acts of the Apostles is one such complexly woven narrative.

Scholars of Acts may debate the number or range of instances in which fittingness or persuasive invention trumps historical 'accuracy' in the narrative, but no credible Acts scholar would say that Luke avoids questions of suitability or idealization altogether. To illustrate this point, consider the following handful of instances in which it is widely agreed that Acts presents idealized portraits rather than portraits guided by concerns for historical accuracy:

1. *The Speeches in Acts.* No ancient writer of history is known to have translated oral speeches verbatim into his historical narratives. Speeches included in ancient narratives were composed according to the criteria of suitability (what a character should say from the historian's perspective) and verisimilitude (what such a character plausibly would say from the historian's perspective) rather than any modern standard of historical accuracy. This is the case even among those who were eyewitness to at least some of the speeches they then transposed into narrative form (the ancient historian, Thucydides, is the classic example here, see below) and also among those who had written copies of speeches in front of them (compare, for instance,

the Septuagint version of biblical speeches with the Jewish historian Josephus's free rewriting of those speeches in his *Antiquities*). The oft-quoted, self-conscious admission of this aspect of the historian's craft comes from Thucydides:

> As for all the things that each side said in speech, either when they were going to war or when they were already in it, it was difficult both for me in the case of things I heard myself and for those who reported to me from various different places to remember exactly the accurate content of the things that were said. *But as it seemed to me*, keeping as closely to the general drift of what truly was said, *that each speaker would most say what was necessary* concerning the always present things, *so I have rendered the speeches* (1.22.1 [trans. Moles]; my emphasis).

Thucydides openly admits that he has crafted the speeches according to what he determines to be 'most necessary' for the speaker to have said. In the mid-twentieth century, the biblical scholar, Martin Dibelius, made the argument that the speeches in Acts were composed by the author according to this same principle, an argument that is almost universally held among Acts scholars. Speeches in Acts seem to be constructed so that what is 'most necessary', according to Lukan theology, comes to be said. Consider, for instance, how the author situates speeches at important turning points in the narrative: (1) the speech of Stephen before his martyrdom, an event which closes the Jerusalem section of Acts and propels the mission into the Gentile world (7.2–8.53); (2) Peter's speech at the conversion of Cornelius, providing rationale for the opening of the mission to the Gentiles (10.34-43); (3) Paul's speech in Athens, the center of polytheistic cultural life and site of the persecution of Socrates, the greatest Greek philosopher (17.22-31); (4) Paul's speech at Miletus at the close of his missionary activity among the Gentiles and before his departure to Jerusalem, where he will be arrested (20.18-35); (5) the series of speeches Paul makes in his defense before the Jews and before governors and kings (beginning in 22.3-21).

One clue that these are literary compositions rather than historical transcripts is the common pattern of 'incompleteness' found in the speeches delivered before crowds. In nearly every instance of speech before a large crowd, the speaker is interrupted before he is able to give his summary statement (this conclusion is made on the principle that repeated patterns in narratives are results of literary stylization rather than historical coincidence). More significantly, as

Dibelius notes, in each of these instances the speech reaches beyond the immediate situation to make larger points that the author himself wishes to stress concerning a matter at hand. These include the major themes of the book: the depravity of non-believing Jews, the terms of Gentile inclusion, the penetration of Christianity into the heart of Greek culture, Paul's heroic biography, Paul's innocence of all charges of wrongdoing, the significance of Jewish rejection of the gospel.

2. *Harmonious Order among Peter, James and Paul.* Reading Paul's canonical letters provides a window into passionate quarrels among early Jesus believers, within which Paul lobs some fairly angry salvos. For example, consider Paul's acerbic wish in Galatians 5.12, in the midst of a quarrel over the significance of circumcision, that his opponents castrate themselves; or his casting of opponents in 2 Corinthians 11.3 as 'Eve' seduced by Satan. On the basis of these epistles alone, it seems that some of these quarrels were not quickly resolved in Paul's favor.

One instance of a rift between Paul and the Jerusalem leadership—especially between Paul and Peter and James—is evident from Galatians 2. In this letter, Paul recounts a meeting with the Jerusalem pillars (Peter, James and John) not long after his conversion. In that encounter agreement is reached that Paul is entrusted with the gospel to the Gentiles, while Peter is entrusted with the gospel to the 'circumcised' (Gal. 2.7-9). By the time Paul writes to the Galatians, however, that agreement has collapsed, owing to a famous early Christian 'food fight' in Antioch; Paul is not only on the outs with James, who does not approve of table fellowship between Jewish Jesus believers and Gentile converts, but he has also become furious with Peter, whom Paul admonishes as a hypocrite for refusing that table fellowship in Antioch when people associated with 'the James party' arrive on the scene. This letter gives no indication that the issue has been resolved by the time Paul writes to the Galatians. He drops the narrative about the controversy abruptly after recalling how he challenged Peter for his hypocrisy. Furthermore, extra-biblical writings continue to suggest that division among various early Christian factions who claimed loyalty to 'Peter', 'James' or 'Paul' persisted into the second century and beyond. (This hostility is especially evident in the extra-canonical *Pseudo-Clementine* literature.)

Acts 15 recounts a version of the so-called Jerusalem Council that bears some similarity to the version of that meeting recounted by Paul in Galatians 2. But Acts idealizes these relationships: both Paul's hostile tone and the impression that unfinished quarrels are still reverberating within the Jesus movement are absent from the Acts account. To be sure, the author of Acts acknowledges that there was deliberation among Peter, James and Paul concerning the significance of circumcision, along with the larger question of law observance among the Gentiles (Acts 15.1-35; cf. also Acts 11), but after a series of measured and orderly speeches, the apostles and the elders, along with the entire Jerusalem church, are said to reach consensus on the matter. A delegation is then appointed to bring this news to Paul and Barnabas in Antioch. The message is received with much rejoicing and the delegates are sent off in peace. Acts here seems to be giving the early Jesus movement a makeover, such that its divisions are submerged and the movement conforms to Greco-Roman ideals of harmonious and orderly political deliberation. One striking aspect to this makeover is that Peter, not Paul, is actually assigned the original mission to the uncircumcised in Acts; Peter even articulates a rationale for the Gentile mission that lines up precisely with Paul's own view (compare the direct contrast between Gal. 2.7-8 and Acts 15.7; consider also Peter's long 'Pauline-like' speech justifying Gentile inclusion at Acts 11.4-17). Again, such harmonious points of view seem to owe much more to the author's understanding that a suitable narrative of his emerging social group should signal harmony, rather than to a concern to present the more historical situation of early Christian disagreement, multiple voices and widely divergent perspectives.

3. *Paul's Triple Pedigree.* In his own epistles, Paul speaks of having lived as a Pharisee (Phil. 3.5; cf. Gal. 1.14) and, thus, as a member of a Jewish party known for guarding ancestral customs and for rigorous adherence to the law. In Acts, this Pharisaic pedigree is enhanced by the assertion that Paul was no ordinary Pharisee, but received exceptional training in Pharisaic ways through sitting at the feet of the highly regarded Jewish teacher, Gamaliel, in Jerusalem (22.3). But the Paul of Acts is not exceptional merely because of his Pharisaic identity. In an exchange with a Roman tribune while he is in custody, the Paul of Acts asserts that he is also a citizen of the Greek city of Tarsus in Cilicia (21.39), a city that rivaled Athens and Alexandria as a center of Greek learning in the first century of the Common Era. Finally, the Paul of Acts is depicted as a Roman citizen, and this citizenship is further qualified as having been acquired by inheritance, rather than through purchase (22.25-28; compare also 16.37-38); the latter was a more popular, and, hence, somewhat vulgar, means of acquiring citizenship during the reign of the emperor Claudius.

How to assess these large and somewhat conflicting claims that Paul was a Jerusalem-trained Pharisee of the Pharisees, a full citizen of a glorious Greek city and a Roman citizen by birth to boot? We need not doubt that Paul affiliated with Pharisees for at least a portion of his life (though the epistles suggest that identity is not retained after his dramatic encounter with the risen Christ). It is not absolutely impossible that a Jew of Tarsus could have been a citizen of that city (though such a citizen would have been counted among the most elite residents of the city, a status that does not fit with the claim that Paul worked as a tentmaker [Acts 18.3]). Nor is it out of the realm of possibility that a diaspora Jew in the middle of the first century could have held Roman citizenship. Each identity claim, standing on its own, while not plausible, is possible. What strains credulity to the breaking point is the idea that Paul could have held each of these three highly coveted status markers—a Pharisee trained in Jerusalem by Gamaliel, a full citizen of the Greek city of Tarsus and a Roman citizen by birth—simultaneously.

For the citizenship claims to be credible, Paul would have to have been born into one of the most elite governing families of Tarsus. But where evidence of highborn Jews entering into full citizenship of a Greek city occurs, it is accompanied by signs of assimilation or integration into Greek customs. Pharisees, by contrast, are noted for zealous adherence to particular Jewish practices, a position that is quite the opposite of assimilation and accommodation to non-Jewish culture. Luke's overriding concern here seems not to be with providing historically accurate data concerning Paul's pedigree, but with asserting, in every instance and within every social circumstance, that Paul is simply among 'the best of the best' with regard to education, piety, wealth and status.

4. *The Eloquence and Heroism of Paul.* We have already made reference to Paul's occasional resort to vitriol in his own correspondence. Paul's autobiographical references in these epistles also suggest a personal struggle with bodily infirmity (Gal. 4.13-14; 2 Cor. 12.7-10), along with an admittedly weak bodily presence and rhetorical style (2 Cor. 10.10). However, we seem to see a rather different Paul in Acts. After his decision to follow Christ in Acts 9, Paul, in keeping with his idealized pedigree in that book, shows no sign of weakness or lack of self-mastery whatsoever. From the time he takes the center stage in Acts 13, Paul exhibits oratorical finesse, whether he is evangelizing in Pisidian Antioch, vying with philosophers in Athens, bidding farewell to his followers in Miletus or defending himself from baseless charges

cast by enemies in Jerusalem and Caesarea. His piercing intelligence enables him to assess tense situations appropriately and free himself from ever-present danger.

Demonstrating the sort of resilience found among modern day comic book heroes, Paul can be struck down, but never defeated. After Paul is stoned and left for dead in Lystra, he is able to pick himself up and travel off to Derbe without even a day for recuperation (14.19-21). After a severe flogging, he spends his night in jail singing hymns and is ready to continue evangelizing immediately on escaping from prison (16.22-40). On the island of Malta, he survives a snakebite that would have sent an ordinary mortal to his grave (28.3-6).

Perhaps the act of heroism that resonates most with the escapades of protagonists in comic book adventures is his absolute command in the shipwreck scene in Acts 27. Surviving a suspenseful shipwreck was a common trope in the ancient novel and Luke employs the trope here to depict Paul in a heroic light. Paul has the prescience to know that the travel ahead will be dangerous and that cargo and even lives could be lost (27.9-10). Once the predicted trouble comes upon them, Paul takes charge, instructing the ship's crew on how to save the passengers from death (vv. 21-26) and, later, administering food rations (vv. 33-38). His careful management of the situation leads the ship to a safe port. After surviving the snakebite in Malta, he heals many on the island from their infirmities. Paul's authoritative stance in this scene and the deference which is granted to him by all parties he encounters, belie the fact that he is in Roman custody throughout the entire adventure.

Conclusion

Two overarching principles guiding ancient authors of historical narrative, including the author of Acts, are (1) imitation of previous models; and (2) idealization in the service of crafting suitable prose. Thus, as the author crafts his story for Theophilus with an eye to providing truth or surety, he is careful to underscore that events in Acts are recognizable according to literary precedents (including the Septuagint and also Greek models found in drama, epic, philosophical treatises, etc.). He is also careful to present the behaviors of his protagonists in exemplary fashion, so that they too may serve as models worthy of imitation. The idealization of the apostle Paul, the chief protagonist from Acts 13 onward, raises the question of how the Acts narrative relates to the Pauline epistles, our other text base for reconstructing the Paul of history. To this discussion, we now turn.

Acts and the Pauline Corpus

If one were using broad brush strokes, it would be possible to paint the Paul presented in his own letters and the Paul depicted in Acts in identical hues. (I follow scholarly convention in assuming that Paul authored the following epistles: Romans, 1 and 2 Corinthians, Galatians, Philippians, 1 Thessalonians and Philemon and that other letters in the canon attributed to Paul are pseudonymous.) Both of these textual traditions concur that Paul first persecuted followers of Jesus, but that, through divine intervention, his outlook changed dramatically, such that he became a zealous promoter of the movement he once attempted to extinguish. Both traditions also concur that at some time after this change of outlook, Paul communicated with leaders from Jerusalem, including James and Peter, and that the communication involved the terms of entry for Gentiles into the fellowship of the Jesus believing group (the *ekklēsia*), especially regarding the question of circumcision and dietary laws. Both describe Paul as traveling considerable distances between major cities of the Roman Empire (primarily those on the Aegean coastline) and engaging with other Jesus believers in those cities.

But anyone seeking a more detailed portrait than these three broad strokes will not be able to dip their brushes quite so readily into both cans of paint. Aside from these three basic points of agreement, the differences between the two portraits range far and wide and pertain to basic questions of Paul's identity, the manner in which he communicates, the audience to whom he communicates, his relationship to other leaders within the assembly, along with the theological/political crux of his message. These differences will be considered more than once in this guide as we seek to understand the book of Acts more deeply. A number of them are highlighted here as a means to indicate their scope.

First, and perhaps most remarkably, the Paul who is famous for authoring letters to churches from Galatia to Rome (and to whom many more letters are attributed, both within and outside of the canon), is never once described in Acts as having written a letter. Nor do the assemblies with whom he engages in Acts ever once refer to having received any such letters. The Paul of Acts does not write letters; he is rather a consummate orator, always taking the upper hand in any situation of open debate, whether in the synagogue or before political officials.

This depiction of Paul as a skilled public speaker in Acts sets up a contrast with the Pauline epistles that goes well beyond what we might think of as the difference between oral and written speech in a modern context. As the classicist, Maude Gleason, reminds us of the historical period under consideration, rhetoric was the means by which elite men of the city forged their manhood. Gleason stresses the physicality of ancient oratorical performance, going so far as to dub such performance a 'calisthenics of manhood' (Gleason 1995: xxii). She offers the following vivid details as part of the ancient oratorical experience:

> ... the sheer sweat of exertion involved in projecting an unamplified voice before a large outdoor audience, the demands of managing the heavy folds of the cloak or toga, the exhilarating risk of stumbles and solecisms lying in wait for a moment's loss of nerve, the vibrant immediacy of a collaborative live audience, ready to explode with jeers or applause (Gleason 1995: xx).

Thus, Acts' characterization of Paul as a skilled orator is an assertion of high status and also of a muscularity that is dramatically out of sync with Paul's own references to his bodily weakness and infirmity. Consider, for example, his concession in his letters: to his weak bodily presence and his inconsequential speech (2 Cor. 10.10); to the weakness stemming from the 'thorn in the flesh' (2 Cor. 12.7-10); to the physical infirmity he bore when preaching the Gospel in Galatia (Gal. 4.13-14); or his own derogatory self-assessment, which culminates in the assertion that he and his companions are no more than the garbage of the world (1 Cor. 4.8-13).

These two dueling portraits of Paul's bodily presence in the epistles versus Acts—which we may characterize in terms of femininity/weakness on the one hand, and masculinity/strength on the other—also correspond to two distinct and competing theological foci, traditionally characterized as the epistles' 'theology of the cross' versus Acts' 'theology of glory'. In the Corinthian correspondence especially, Paul engages in a paradoxical embrace of the foolishness of the cross as the sign of God's wisdom, so much so that he decides to know nothing among the Corinthians but Christ, 'and him, crucified'. He downplays the significance of spiritual gifts and particularly those of miraculous demonstrations (1 Cor. 2.2-5). In other words, he revels in his own debasement. Acts, in contrast, speaks little of the cross except when accusing Jews of having crucified Jesus; it highlights instead the wonderworking abilities of the apostles and of Paul, whose miraculous powers are such that even articles of cloth that touch him become agents of healing in and of themselves (19.12). In short, in his letters, Paul is weak and glories in that weakness as a sign of the crucified Christ living in him. In Acts, Paul is remarkably—one might say, gloriously—strong, with a message focusing much more on resurrection/vindication than on any shameful connotation of crucifixion.

One could also identify the contrast between these two textual bases in terms of politics by noting that Paul's epistles suggest that his ministry is counter-cultural in a way that threatens the 'rulers of this age', while Acts depicts his ministry as politically safe. Many biblical scholars interested in claiming Paul as an advocate of political resistance to empire—including Richard Horsley (2000), Sze-Kar Wan (2000), Davina Lopez (2008), Neil Elliot (2008) and Brigitte Kahl (2010)—note that to embrace 'the foolishness of the cross', as Paul does in his own letters, is to radically revalue (and, hence, to subvert) this Roman symbol of extreme degradation and torture. Passages from the Pauline epistles to which these scholars point in order to make the case that Paul has an anti-Roman political edge include: 1 Thess. 5.1-11, which is cast as Paul's challenge to the Roman ideology of 'peace and security'; 1 Cor. 15.24-28, in which Paul's assertion that Christ subjects every ruler and authority to God's own rule is read as a dismissal of Roman rule; Phil. 3.19-21, which describes an alternate politics, constitution and citizenship for members of the assembly; and large portions of Galatians (especially Gal. 3:28), which is read as part of a movement for 'international solidarity' among the nations that have been defeated by the Roman Empire. They note that Paul's collection for the poor in Jerusalem (see Galatians 2; 2 Corinthians 8 and 9), which is an integral part of Paul's ministry, might also have raised suspicion as an 'alternative tax' distributed to those in need in a territory considered by Romans as a seat of rebellion. The argument that the historical Paul's ministry did, indeed, contain a politically subversive edge is strengthened by the fact that Acts includes accusations of political subversion directed against Paul (16.20-21; 17.6-7; 18.13; 19.25-27; 24.5). Acts knows the charges and openly raises them against Paul, but only to refute them by offering a counter narrative of a ministry which poses no threat to empire.

Consider also the issue of Paul's identity and authority. Paul, in his own letters, repeatedly refers to himself as an apostle and engages in several defenses of his authority as an apostle. (As a sampling, consider Rom. 1.1, Galatians and 1 Corinthians, especially the following: 1 Cor. 4.9 'For I think that God has exhibited us apostles as last of all, as though sentenced to death, because we have become a spectacle to the world'; 1 Cor. 15.9, 'For I am the least of the apostles.' See also 2 Cor. 11:5, 'I think that I am not in the least inferior to these super-apostles.') Acts, in contrast, prefers to reserve the title of apostle for the Twelve, who are set apart in Jerusalem and qualified for this role on account of their relationship with Jesus before the crucifixion (1.21-26). While Acts preserves two indirect references to Paul as an apostle (14.4, 14), Paul's apostleship is never foregrounded as an integral aspect of his identity. It is never mentioned in his own speeches, not even in those which are most autobiographical. It is never a topic of debate.

This apostleship is further qualified as an apostleship to the Gentiles in Paul's epistles and, in line with that qualification, Paul's letters are addressed to those within Jesus believing communities which seem to be composed primarily, if not exclusively, of Gentile converts. Never in his letters does he mention entering a synagogue, much less engaging in heated debates within any synagogue. While Acts also identifies Paul as being set apart for the Gentiles, Acts, in distinction to the epistles, underscores that the Gentile mission is tied integrally to a companion ministry to Jews. In the Acts narrative, Paul always speaks first in the synagogue and only then (usually after Jewish rejection) does he move to Gentile audiences.

Further discrepancies concern both Paul's allies and his opponents. Paul's most heated arguments within his letters are with other Jesus believers: those who interpret the consequences of Jesus belief differently from him. (The rhetoric of Galatians, along with 1 and 2 Corinthians, is especially combative, though Philippians and Romans also contain signs of some intense intramural dispute.) Only once, in 1 Thess. 2.14-16, does the question of extramural Jewish hostility come up; yet even this hostility is depicted as having been addressed to Jesus believers in Judea *as an analogy for* the hostility confronting the Thessalonian Jesus believers by their Gentile neighbors and not as an instance of Jewish hostility directed against Paul or his churches. (It may be, further, noted that a number of biblical scholars regard 1 Thess. 2.14-16 as a later, non-Pauline interpolation, as it seems to express a theology most common among Christian texts dated after the Jewish war.) In contrast, Acts minimizes intramural quarrels among Jesus believers and depicts non-believing Jews as the chief agents in hostility against Paul: they are maniacally fixed upon Paul's destruction.

In short, Acts' portrait of Paul departs at significant junctures from his self-portrait. How might one account for this? Biblical traditionalists who require that scriptures provide an unshakable historical foundation must, of course, deny that these differences are irreconcilable. Another solution within circles of historical-critical biblical scholarship has been to excuse Acts' departures from the epistles by arguing that the author of Acts does not have access to the Pauline epistles; he is, therefore, working from variant oral traditions and written sources, rather than the epistles themselves. A third way to account for the discrepancies is to understand the author of Acts as motivated by the criteria of suitability and persuasiveness, which, as noted above, are chief concerns for ancient authors of historical narrative. An author motivated by these criteria might, indeed, have known and read Paul's epistles, but this would not require him (as it would the modern historian) to construct a biography that would correlate closely with this source.

The author of Acts constructs Paul according to his own vision of the early Jesus movement and in line with the concerns of his own community; this is not unlike the way that the Gospel authors adapt the message of Jesus so that it speaks to the concerns of their respective time and situation. This raises the question of when the book of Acts was written, to which we now turn.

Dating Acts

By scholarly convention, Acts is dated to the late 80s or early 90s of the Common Era. The assumptions guiding this conventional dating include: (1) Mark is the earliest canonical Gospel, written sometime close to the destruction of Jerusalem (c. 70 CE); (2) the Gospel of Luke depends on Mark, and, therefore, must have been composed later (c. 80 CE); and (3) Acts is a lengthy second volume that would have taken some years to complete beyond the finish date for the Gospel of Luke (c. 85-90 CE). Since Acts makes no reference to Pauline letters (which began to circulate in Christian communities as a collection by the early second century, if not the late first century) and does not acknowledge Paul's execution (a trauma that was widely known by the early second century), scholars are inclined to push Acts' composition to no later than the end of the first century.

A recent cluster of scholarship challenges this conventional dating by pushing the completion of Acts into the early second century, possibly as late as 125 or 130 CE. (This position was already articulated in the mid-twentieth century by the biblical scholar, John Knox.) These scholars note the following arguments in support of their position:

1. Christian authors of the early and mid-second century did know and quote many biblical texts, but they did not quote the Acts of the Apostles. The first Christian who clearly employs the book of Acts in his own writings is Irenaeus, whose treatise against heresy is dated to 180 CE.

2. Acts appears to rely on passages from Book 18 of the *Jewish Antiquities*, which was written by Josephus around 95 CE.

3. While Acts does not make explicit reference to the Pauline letter collection and does not construct a Pauline biography that is consistent with Paul's autobiographical reflections, it does seem to be working, however loosely, from that letter collection.

4. Acts seems more attuned to issues that plagued the church in the second century rather than the first. This text draws distinctions between Jews and Christians as two separate religious groups, attempts to shore up the author's own group from Christians he views as dissenters (see the caution against the 'savage wolves' and the reference to 'overseers' or 'bishops' [*episkopoi*] appointed to guard the flock in Acts 20.27-30) and employs the sorts of arguments in defense of Christianity that are also used by second century apologists. Acts also uses the word 'Christian' to name its group, a term that otherwise appears only in texts from the second century (11.26; 26.28).

Readers seeking a basic overview of Acts from this book will not need to make a decision about the date of Acts' composition before moving forward. For the sake of disclosure, however, let me note that I have thrown my hat in with those who push Acts to a later time (i.e. around 125 CE). This time period seems to illuminate best the issues the author of Acts raises and the solutions he proposes. This is so especially regarding three questions: Acts and cultural security under empire, Acts and 'the Jews', and, finally, Acts and emerging intra-Christian debates. Some of these second-century concerns will be taken up again in greater length in the chapters to come. But before we examine these particular themes, we turn, in the next chapter, to an overview of the narrative.

For Further Reading

Alexander, Loveday
2006   *Acts in its Ancient Literary Context* (New York/London: T. & T. Clark International).
Aune, David E.
1987   *The New Testament in its Literary Environment* (Philadelphia, PA: Westminster John Knox Press).
Balch, David L.
1989   'Comments on the Genre and a Political Theme of Luke–Acts: A Preliminary Comparison of Two Hellenistic Historians', in *SBL Seminar Papers* (SBLSP, 28; Atlanta, GA: Scholars Press), pp. 343-61.
Barrett, C.K.
1961   *Luke the Historian in Recent Study* (London: Epworth).
Bonz, Marianne Palmer
2000   *The Past as Legacy: Luke–Acts and Ancient Epic* (Minneapolis, MN: Fortress Press).
Cancik, Hubert
1997   'The History of Culture, Religion and Institutions in Ancient Historiography: Philological Observations Concerning Luke's History', *Journal of Biblical Literature* 116, pp. 673-95.
Conzelmann, Hans
1987   *Acts of the Apostles* (Hermeneia; Philadelphia, PA: Fortress Press).
Dibelius, Martin
1956   *Studies in the Acts of the Apostles* (London: SCM Press).
Dupertuis, Ruben
2005   'The Summaries of Acts 2,4, and 5 and Plato's Republic', in *Ancient Fiction: The Matrix of Early Christian and Jewish Narrative* (ed. Jo-Ann A. Brant, Charles W. Hedrick, and Chris Shea; Atlanta, GA: Society of Biblical Literature), pp. 275-95.

Elliot, Neil

2008   *The Arrogance of Nations* (Minneapolis, MN: Fortress Press).

Gleason, Maude

1995   *Making Men: Sophists and Self-Presentation in Ancient Rome* (Princeton, NJ: Princeton University Press).

Horsley, Richard (ed.)

2000   *Paul and Politics* (Harrisburg, PA: Trinity Press International).

Kahl, Brigitte

2010   *Galatians Re-imagined: Reading with the Eyes of the Vanquished* (Minneapolis, MN: Fortress Press).

Konstan, David

1998   'The Invention of Fiction', in *Ancient Fiction and Early Christian Narrative* (ed. Ronald Hock, J. Bradley Chance, Judith Perkins; Atlanta, GA: Scholars Press), pp. 3-17.

Lopez, Davina C.

2008   *Apostle to the Conquered: Reimagining Paul's Mission* (Minneapolis, MN: Fortress Press).

Penner, Todd

2004   *In Praise of Christian Origins: Stephen and the Hellenists in Lukan Apologetic Historiography* (New York: T. & T. Clark International).

Pervo, Richard

2006   *Dating Acts: Between the Evangelists and the Apologists* (Santa Rosa, CA: Polebridge).

1987   *Profit with Delight: The Literary Genre of the Acts of the Apostles* (Philadelphia, PA: Fortress Press).

Smith, Abraham

1995   'A Second Step in African Biblical Interpretation: A Generic Reading Analysis of Acts 8:26-40', in *Reading from this Place. I. Social Location and Biblical Interpretation in the United States* (ed. Fernando F. Segovia and Mary Ann Tolbert; Minneapolis, MN: Fortress Press), pp. 213-28.

Sterling, Gregory E.

1992   *Historiography and Self-Definition: Josephus, Luke–Acts and Apologetic Historiography* (Leiden: Brill).

Talbert, Charles H.

1974   *Literary Patterns, Theological Themes and the Genre of Luke–Acts* (Missoula, MT: Scholars Press).

Tannehill, Robert C.

1986–1994   *The Narrative Unity of Luke-Acts: A Literary Interpretation* (2 vols.; Philadelphia, PA, and Minneapolis, MN: Fortress Press).

Wan, Sze-Kar

2000   'Collection for the Saints as Anticolonial Act', in Horsley (2000), pp. 191-215.

2

NARRATIVE OVERVIEW

The twenty-eight chapters of Acts cover an enormous amount of territory, both geographically and thematically. This chapter organizes the text of Acts, chapter by chapter, under four subdivisions and provides a brief summary and analysis of each in order to assist the reader in identifying the general structure of the plot, along with some of the major themes Luke wishes to underscore as the story unfolds. As in the previous chapter, so here, the overview assumes that the text of Acts is a rhetorical argument, asserting, in the midst of contest, one particular narrative of the emergence of the Jesus movement, focused on a particular geographic region. Thus, we consider not merely the narrative, but also gaps in the narrative—hints of other stories that could be told, of other Christianities also emerging, of voices telling another story than the one preserved by Luke. These four subdivisions are: (1) The Jerusalem section, 1.1–8.3; (2) The transition from the ministry of the Jerusalem leaders to the mission of the apostle Paul, 8.4–12.25; (3) Paul's Gentile mission, 13.1–20.38; and (4) Paul in Roman custody, 21.1–28.31.

The Jerusalem Section, Acts 1.1–8.3

Jerusalem is the climactic destination for Jesus in the Third Gospel and in this second volume the city's centrality continues to be underscored. The first seven chapters of Acts are set entirely within this city's walls. After the preface, which invokes Theophilus again as the patron for these two volumes (Acts 1.1-2; cf. Lk. 1.1-4), Luke reminds readers that the resurrected Jesus had appeared to the disciples in this city and exhorted them to remain there and await the descent of the Holy Spirit. (Luke's restriction of resurrection appearances to Jerusalem stands in tension with the announcement of the angelic being at the tomb in Mk. 16.7 that the resurrected Jesus is going ahead to Galilee and that the disciples should go there to meet him.) The Lukan Jesus' final prophetic words to the disciples before his ascension reveal the universal scope of the mission that the Holy Spirit will inaugurate in this city: 'You will receive power when the Holy Spirit has come upon you; and you will be my witnesses in Jerusalem, in all Judea and Samaria, and to the ends of the earth' (1.8). As the narrative progresses beyond Acts 8, the prophecy of far-reaching travel by the witnesses will be, at least partially, fulfilled. But before Luke takes us out of the city, he narrates a series of foundational events that happen here.

Apostolic Authority

Two of these events have to do with the establishment of leadership for the movement: first, the deliberations over the replacement of Judas among the Twelve (1.15-26); and second, the establishment of 'The Seven' to assist the Twelve in ministry (6.1-6; though the title 'deacon' is not used here, early church tradition identifies these seven as the first to hold this ecclesiastical office). In the unfolding of both of these narratives, Luke delivers on his promise to provide an 'orderly' account. In the first, Judas's act of betrayal, with all of its potentially disturbing theological implications, is reassuringly cast as having been foretold by the scriptures; an orderly process for replacement is then proposed, the piety of the apostles is indicated by their prayerful discernment, divine guidance is secured through the casting of lots. In the second, a hint of dissension might be drawn from the fact that the appointment of the Seven is prompted by complaints or 'murmurings' (*goggusmos*), an allusion to the grumblings of the ungrateful children of Israel under Moses' leadership. But the dissension is quickly resolved. The apostles propose a solution that meets with unanimous approval: a division of labor between the service of the word and that of the table. This decision is formally enacted through the consecration of the Seven.

Readers suspicious about the patriarchal direction taken by the early church in terms of leadership offices might note the androcentric nature of these stories. Peter lays out criteria for Judas's replacement: the candidate must be a man (*anēr*, a gender specific term) who accompanied them until the day Jesus was taken up. Had he used the generic inclusive 'human' (*anthrōpos*), Mary Magdalene might have been the obvious choice; that he didn't might suggest a cover up. Furthermore, though the twelve male apostles consecrate seven males to serve table, we get no more information about those 'widows' who were the source of the dissension in the first place. Extra-biblical traditions about both the leadership of Mary Magdalene among the apostles (see especially the *Gospel of Mary*) and about widows carrying out ecclesiastical duties (see the backhanded acknowledgement of an order of widows in 1 Tim. 5.3-16) remind readers that Luke is not telling the entire story here with regard to women's leadership in the movement.

Pentecost

We will devote the entire last chapter of this guide to a close reading of this pericope. Here only a brief overview is provided. The story of flames descending from heaven and the language miracle on the day of Pentecost (2.1-41) might, at first glance, be considered a disruptive intrusion between the two orderly succession tales we discussed above, but this pericope also comes to orderly resolution. The disruption begins with the descent of the Holy Spirit, prompting a cacophony of voices so that peoples gathered from all corners of the earth are spoken to, each in their own language. From the perspective of outsiders, the language miracle appears as drunkenness. Yet, Peter's subsequent speech provides one, and only one, interpretation of the significance of the language miracle. The speech is met with repentance by thousands, followed by their baptism.The crowd of the baptized turn to an extreme (and orderly) form of piety and ethics, selling their possessions and living communally (2.43-47; cf. the ideal portrait of communal living in 4.32-37).

Peter's interpretation of the language miracle in 2.14-36 articulates a number of themes that will be repeated in speeches throughout the book of Acts. He reminds his Jewish audience that they were responsible for the killing of Jesus, but that God has raised Jesus up to be both Lord and Messiah. He insists that all of this was foretold in the scriptures, offering a string of quotations from the Septuagint as proof. Finally, he exhorts them to repent. This speech is repeated by Peter twice more, with only slight variation, in chapters immediately following, first prompted by the astonishment of the crowd after Peter and John heal a lame man at one of the gates of the Temple (3.11-26), next by hostile questioners who have arrested them (4.8-12). Its basic outline will be employed by Paul in his mission as well.

Divine Intervention

Within these first chapters the power of divine agency to punish those who miss the mark is clearly (and somewhat gruesomely) asserted. We are told that Judas's insides burst open in the midst of a field (1.18); Ananias and Sapphira meet sudden death because they refuse to comply with the prac-tice of turning over all wealth to the common fund (5.1-11). The apostles are also subject to divine intervention, but, in their case, for protection rather than harm. At the arrest of the apostles by the High Priest and his henchmen, an angel of the Lord effects a miraculous prison escape for them (5.17-25). In the next scene, the high-minded Pharisee, Gamaliel, puts into direct speech what the prison escape had illustrated through narration; a plan from God cannot be thwarted by human resistors (5.33-39).

The Stoning of Stephen

The speech of the sage, Gamaliel, does nothing to quell the desire among non-believers in Jerusalem to persecute those who proclaim Jesus as messiah. The final scene in the Jerusalem section of Acts—the trial and execution of Stephen—makes this clear. The witness of the apostles, in powerful words and miraculous deeds, is said to have resulted in the conversion of thousands in Jerusalem to the movement, but it also provokes opposition, including imprisonments (4.3), threats (4.21) and beatings (5.40). The opposition reaches its climax in the stoning of Stephen, the first believer to be killed for his testimony concerning Jesus.

Stephen is confronted by Jerusalem's synagogue affiliates, whose native lands evoke the 'international' scope of the opposition. As with Jesus before him, he is subject to hostile accusations in a juridical context. In his defense, Stephen recites a history of the Israelite ancestors that culminates in the counter charge that his audience killed Jesus. The Christ-killing accusation is starker here than in Peter's many speeches, as it is linked to a long history of prophet killing, thus suggesting that the vice of killing innocents sent by God is congenital. In response, the legal procedure against Stephen degenerates into a mob scene, with the angry crowd rushing him out of the city to kill him. Stephen's ordeal is a pivotal scene for many reasons. For one, it is clearly modeled on the suffering of Jesus (note the three instances in which Stephen's speech echoes Jesus' speech during his passion: Lk. 22.69/Acts 7.56; Lk. 23.46/Acts 7.59; Lk. 23.34a/Acts 7.60). Further, Saul/Paul is introduced here as having approved of the killing (7.58); in a subsequent speech concerning his own 'conversion', Paul will remind readers that he was a witness to this pivotal event (22.17-21). It is also said that Stephen's death ignites a persecution that causes believers to scatter (8.1; cf. 11.19-26); Stephen's death, thus, helps to facilitate the fulfillment of the prophecy in Acts 1.8 that Jesus' witnesses will spread to the ends of the earth. Finally, unlike the death of Jesus and the imprisonment of Paul, it is a violent action that takes place apart from Roman authorities and, as such, unambiguously posits Jews as solely responsible for the first murder of a Jesus believer. The absence of Roman participation in this first martyr's death and the instigation of that death by a mob of angry Jews are narrative details that conform to Luke's overall rhetorical strategy concerning both Romans and Jews: Luke exculpates the former and inculpates the latter. We will analyze this strategy in further detail in subsequent chapters.

Connecting Paul to the Jerusalem Apostles, Acts 8.4–12.25

Paul will soon take center stage as protagonist in Acts and his conversion is already narrated in this transitional section. But included here are also a few narratives concerning other apostles; these serve to invoke a larger mission field than that of Paul's alone, while also paving the way for Paul's mission to the Gentiles. Internal dissension among believers arises again: once in a conflict with a magician whose conversion appears to be inauthentic; a second time within a large assembly of Jerusalem Jesus believers regarding the question of circumcision and the terms of Gentile inclusion. External opposition also threatens and Herod kills an apostle, but such violence serves only as a catalyst for growth. As in the Jerusalem section, persecution is always met by an increase in the number of adherents to the movement and an expanse of the mission's geographical reach.

Simon and the Holy Spirit

In Acts 8, Philip, Peter and John move from Jerusalem into Samaria, proclaiming the word of the Lord and performing miraculous signs. The encounter with Simon in Samaria, who receives the baptism of Jesus Christ but not that of the Holy Spirit, takes up a theme introduced in the Ananias and Sapphira episode: not all purported believers are truly among the saved. As with Ananias and Sapphira, the issue here is wealth. Simon wishes to buy further access to the power of the Holy Spirit. Though he is not stricken dead for his vulgar hope that money can buy this power, Peter suggests that his wickedness may not be forgivable (8.19-22). Here and elsewhere, Acts reminds us that the issue of salvation is not merely one of outsiders-versus-insiders, but also between 'true insiders' and 'false ones'. Baptism in itself appears to be no guarantee of salvation.

Conversion of the Ethiopian Eunuch

For Philip, the most significant encounter is with an Ethiopian court official, whom he baptizes while the official is traveling back to his homeland after visiting Jerusalem (8.26-40). This episode spills over with elements of legend and myth: the officer is reading just the right biblical passage at just the right time when he encounters the missionary; water appears in the desert at the perfect time for a baptism; the Spirit snatches Philip away once the baptism is accomplished and teleports him down the road toward Caesarea. Since, from the perspective of ancient Greek literature, Ethiopia signified 'the ends of the earth', this encounter also underscores the fulfillment of the prophecy in 1.8. Greco-Roman authors idealized Ethiopia as a utopian state, a land of great wealth, military might and wisdom. This conversion of the treasurer of the queen of Ethiopia, like the conversion of the Roman centurion that follows, thus signifies that the Christian message is persuasive to people of high standing from both near and far.

Because this is the only major narrative in Acts concerning an African follower of 'the Way', it also serves to remind readers that this text has been highly selective in the narrative of early Christianity it tells. Here and elsewhere in Acts, we are given glimpses of the embrace of Christianity by Africans (cf. the references in Acts 13.1 to Simeon 'the Black' [*Niger*] and Lucius of Cyrene). Toward the end of the second century and into the third, substantial Christian communities were to be found in Egypt (especially Alexandria, home of Clement and Origen) and Carthage. But while the eunuch is sent on his way home to Ethiopia rejoicing, the narrator does not follow him there to tell any part of the story of African Christianity. Luke will soon turn his attention fully and completely westward, tracing the mission from Jerusalem to Asia Minor to Europe and, ultimately, Rome.

The 'Conversion' of Saul

Meanwhile, Saul/Paul emerges again, as a persecutor of those who belong to 'the Way', until the moment he is struck down and blinded on the road to Damascus. This 'conversion' of Paul is so important to Acts that the narrative will be repeated three times (9.1-22; 22.4-16; 26.9-18). Scholars of the historical Paul, particularly those who embrace the so-called 'new perspective' on Paul, stress that Paul's own understanding of his ministry to the Gentiles, as expressed in his epistles, can best be understood as a prophetic calling rather than as a conversion to a new religion (see, for example, Eisenbaum 2009). But the dramatic nature of the turning, as told in the Acts narrative, suggests that the author of Acts would mark Paul out as having changed profoundly on that road. In Acts, Paul emerges from the experience with a one-hundred-and-eighty-degree turn of mind, now embracing the proclamation of Jesus as Christ with the same zeal he had once shown in persecuting those who so believed. The 'conversion' also transforms Paul from persecutor to persecuted. Immediately after Paul begins proclaiming Jesus, plots are concocted by non-believing Jews to kill him (9.23). Paul will be plagued by such conspirators throughout much of the remaining narrative.

Conversion of Cornelius

In the midst of Paul's conversion story, the Lord speaks to make clear that Paul is the instrument by which his name will be announced to the Gentiles (9.15). We can say that Peter paves the way for that instrumentality through the events concerning the conversion of Cornelius (10.1–11.18). The story involves the terms of Gentile inclusion within the Jesus movement. Since (1) the Jesus movement began as a movement *within* Judaism; (2) the earliest devotees were Jewish; and (3) the movement relied on a particular reading of Jewish scriptures—including the notion of a Jewish messiah being promised in those scriptures—the question of whether a Gentile interested in joining with Christ believers should be required to observe the Jewish law was intensely debated among early followers. The focus of debate centered especially on two issues central to ancient Jewish identity: the observance of dietary laws and circumcision. These questions also animate Paul's letters to the Galatians and the Romans (see especially Gal. 2.1-14). While Paul is the chief spokesperson in Galatians for communal table practice among Jews and Gentiles in Christ, here the revelation comes to Peter in the form of a dream concerning the eating of unclean animals. The meaning of the dream is clarified through his encounter with Cornelius, the Roman centurion in Caesarea; the result is the baptism of a number of Gentiles, Cornelius among them.

A slight hint concerning the controversial nature of the question is given in the note that some of the circumcised believers in Jerusalem criticized Peter for his decision to eat with Cornelius (11.2), to say nothing of the fact that the issue will be raised for a second time in Acts 15. Once again, as we have come to expect, Peter's speech quells the critics. Dissenting opinions dissolve into harmonious praise (11.18).

Violence in Jerusalem

Jerusalem again becomes the scene of persecution in Acts 12, with Herod killing James, the brother of John, and putting Peter in prison. (The Herod in question here is Agrippa I, the grandson of Herod the Great, who is infamous in biblical narrative for implementing the slaughter of the innocents in Bethlehem, according to Matthew 2.) Themes that arise here are familiar from previous chapters: violence against believers in Jesus is spurred on by the Jews (cf. 12.3); apostles are persecuted in ways that echo the passion of Jesus (cf. Peter's imprisonment in 12.3, which like that of Jesus before him, occurs during the Passover season); a divinely instigated miraculous prison escape proves that the movement is of God and cannot be thwarted (cf. 5.39); the evil doer is destroyed (cf. 1.18-19).

Paul's Gentile Mission, Acts 13.1–20.38

If you have not yet done so, at this point it would be good to get out a map of the Mediterranean region during the Roman period and acquire some sense of the geographic setting of this section of Acts, for it is here that Paul's three missionary journeys, from the east coast of the Mediterranean to points westward, are charted. The first and shortest journey, narrated in Acts 13-14, begins in Antioch on a sea route around the island of Cyprus and on to Perga on the coast of Asia Minor; it then moves inward on a land route to Pisidian Antioch, with further excursions inward to Iconium, Lystra and Derbe, before returning by sea to Caesarian Antioch. The second and third journeys (15.36–18.22; 18.23–20.36) overlap and cover a much larger swath of territory, including land routes through Asia Minor, along with stops at several major cities in the Aegean basin, including Ephesus, Philippi, Thessalonica and Corinth.

In this section, Lukan artistry is on prominent display. On the one hand, he continues to repeat themes already introduced in previous sections and signal parallelism between Paul and previous protagonists as a means of asserting the coherence and stability of the movement. On the other hand, he employs variation and local color in each specific episode to construct a suspenseful and pleasurable narrative.

Paul before the Proconsul and against the Magician

Saul is introduced in this section as among the prophets and teachers of the church in Antioch. Along with Barnabas, he receives special commendation from the Holy Spirit. (From 13.9 onward, he will only be referred to as Paul, though no explicit reason for the name switch is given.) As Peter before him attracted the attention of the high-ranking Roman official, Cornelius, so, on the island of Cyprus, Paul meets the Roman proconsul, Sergius Paulus, who becomes a believer after seeing the 'teachings of the Lord' in action (13.12). (Though it must be said that Paul's convert is even more prestigious than Peter's: the claim that a Roman bearing the office of proconsul—one who had served as a consul and then, on senatorial appointment, received the governorship of a province—is a remarkably audacious assertion by Luke of the influence of Paul in the highest circles of Roman society.) As Peter had encountered and defeated Simon Magus, so Paul gives the magician Bar-Jesus/Elymas his comeuppance. Then, with his companions, he leaves Cyprus to journey to Asia Minor.

Paul among Jews and Gentile Sympathizers on his Missionary Journeys

The first Pauline missionary encounter narrated at any length is set in Pisidian Antioch; the many details given here might be taken as paradigmatic for Paul's encounters with Jews and Gentiles in these regions. First, it is said that Paul begins his mission in the city's synagogue, where he is invited to preach. The sermon, echoing sermons of Peter in Jerusalem, involves quotations from the Septuagint, insists that these scriptures point to Jesus as messiah, reminds that Jesus was unjustly killed by residents of Jerusalem, proclaims triumphantly Jesus' vindication through the resurrection and calls for repentance. Some Jews are persuaded, as are many Gentiles, but many Jews are not persuaded, prompting Paul's declaration that he will now turn to the Gentiles (13.46-47); non-believing Jews subsequently incite violent resistance to the Pauline mission. Variations on this pattern of (1) Paul's preaching in the synagogue; (2) successful conversion of some Jews; (3) violent responses of non-believing Jews (who often incite Gentiles to violence as well); and (4) successful conversions of Gentiles in spite of this violence, will follow in Lystra and Derbe (14.19-28), Thessalonica (17.1-9), Beroea (17.10-15) and Corinth (18.1-17).

Paul's 'missionary two-step' in Acts, of preaching first in synagogues to the Jews and then moving on to the Gentiles outside of the synagogue, stands in tension with Paul's own epistles in which he describes himself solely as an 'apostle to the Gentiles' and never mentions entering a diaspora synagogue to address a Jewish audience. Most Pauline scholars explain this tension by suggesting the synagogue visit as part of Luke's tendency to narrativize Pauline theological claims. In Paul's letter to the Romans he argues repeatedly that Jews have priority with regard to the Gospel and that Gentiles received it only secondarily (e.g. see Rom. 1.16: 'For I am not ashamed of the gospel; it is the power of God for salvation to everyone who has faith, to the Jew first and also to the Greek'; cf. Rom. 2.9-10; 9.4-5). In his narrative, Luke translates that theological claim into literal movements by Paul, who first enters into the synagogue to address Jews, and then turns to Gentiles. We shall consider the larger question of Acts and the Jews in a separate chapter. Here, as we consider Paul's mission among Jews and sympathetic Gentiles, a few of the ways in which Acts complicates the two-step pattern of preaching *first* to the Jews and *second* to Gentiles are worthy of note.

First, note that Paul's audiences in the synagogue frequently include not only Jews, but also pious Gentiles who attend synagogue and have familiarity with Jewish scripture and sympathy for Jewish practice. Acts generally refers to this group of Gentile sympathizers as 'God-fearers' (*phoboumenoi* and *sebomenoi*). In one instance the God-fearers are referred to as 'proselytes' (13.43a), but more often these Gentiles are depicted as having sympathy for Judaism without having undergone conversion (cf. 13.16, 26, 50; 14.1; 16.14; 17.4; 17.12, 17; 18.4). With only one exception, in the case of the God-fearing women of Pisidian Antioch at 13.50, the God-fearers are depicted as particularly receptive to Paul's missionary preaching, much in the way that Cornelius, the archetypal Gentile convert and also a God-fearer (10.2, 22), was receptive to Peter's message. Thus, these God-fearers function as a narrative device, demonstrating how an intermediary group— part Jew, part Gentile—helped to facilitate the transfer of the gospel of salvation from Jews to Gentiles.

Second, note that tension exists between the author's desire to mark Christians as distinct from Jews on the one hand, and his desire to assert that Christians are, indeed, themselves *true* Jews on the other, as both the narrative of Paul's mission in Corinth (18.1-18) and Apollos's reception in Ephesus (18.24-28) demonstrate. In Corinth, elements that are formulaic—Paul's preaching in the synagogue, followed by Jewish resistance and pronouncement of a turn to the Gentiles—might lead readers to suppose that Paul will now cut ties completely with the non-believing Jewish community there. However, subsequent details prove otherwise. After Paul shakes the dust from his clothes at 'the Jews' and pronounces blood guilt upon them (18.6), he does not settle far off, but rather moves to a house that is 'next door to the synagogue' (18.7), whereupon a leading (presumably, Jewish) synagogue official immediately converts (18.8). In a similarly complex entanglement, Apollos publically and powerfully refutes 'the Jews' in Ephesus (18.28), but only after he himself is first introduced as a Jew who is immersed (literally, 'strong') in Jewish scripture (18.24). As we shall explore at greater length in a subsequent chapter, the author of Acts wishes to distinguish followers of 'the Way' from non-believing Jews in some regards, but not without taking a good number of Jews and 'Jewish things' with him.

The Jerusalem Council (or the Defense of the Pauline Mission by Peter and James)

Acts 15 is devoted to the question of terms for Gentile inclusion within the Jesus movement; it is a more formal enactment of decisions already reached, in Acts 11, by the Jerusalem church in response to the issues of table fellowship and circumcision raised by the conversion of Cornelius and other Gentiles in Caesarea. A key difference between Acts 11 and Acts 15 is that in this second discussion of Gentile inclusion, Paul is present, having been appointed, along with Barnabas, to discuss this matter with the apostles and elders in Jerusalem (15.2). As with Acts 11, dissension is resolved through deliberation which leads to unanimity and formal procedures for communicating that unanimity. Rejoicing, peace and proclamation follow.

One intriguing aspect of this narration of the Jerusalem council is that while Paul is reported to have spoken twice during the deliberations (15.4, 12), none of these words are recorded. Instead, the role of arguing in direct speech for the merits of Gentile inclusion without strict adherence to Mosaic law (i.e. the work of establishing the legitimacy of the Pauline mission) falls first to Peter in establishing the divine will concerning the Gentile mission (15.7-11) and then, to James, who proposes a minimum set of observances required of Gentile converts (15.13-21).

Some scholars explain the roles of Peter and James here as part of Luke's defense of Paul. In contemporary Christianity (and especially in Protestant circles), the apostle Paul might be understood as *the* great hero of the faith who stands next to Jesus himself in stature. But this authority did not adhere to Paul from the beginning. We know, from extra-canonical sources (especially the Pseudo-Clementine literature, a collection of writings dating from the late second through the early fifth century), that Paul was criticized in some early Christian circles both as too radical in his mission to the Gentiles and as one who did not have true apostolic standing. Unlike the disciples who followed Jesus during his ministry in Galilee, Paul did not know Jesus in the flesh or receive an earthly commission from Jesus before his ascension. To be sure, some early Christians embraced Paul for just this reason—but these were Christians who also wanted to argue that Christianity had nothing at all to do with Judaism (and not even with the twelve apostles, since these apostles were Jewish). In this view, the book of Acts is a compromise document, in which Luke 'rescues' Paul from those who critiqued him as too radical in his mission to the Gentiles on the one hand, and from those who celebrated him as having nothing to do with Judaism on the other. Luke does this by not only celebrating Paul's Gentile mission, but also by demonstrating that this Gentile mission is authorized by the foremost of Jewish leaders in Jerusalem: Peter and James.

Paul in Gentile Territory

While stories of Paul's encounters with Jews and God-fearers in synagogues during his missionary journeys adhere to a general pattern, as noted above, these formulaic episodes are interlaced with a more variegated set of stories concerning Paul's encounters with Gentile residents, including Roman officials, on their own turf.

Sandwiched between the violent persecution incited by Jews in Pisidian Antioch and in Lystra is a story of Paul healing a lame man (14.8-18; cf. the parallel with Peter in 3.1-8) and the response of the crowd to the miracle; they mistake Paul and Barnabas for gods and rush to make sacrifice. The scene is certainly a rebuke of pagan piety, in terms of sacrificial practice, polytheism and the quick propensity to worship humans as gods. It may also be understood as poking a bit of fun at the Lystran yokels for their gullibility.

In Philippi, Paul also encounters a degraded form of Gentile religious practice, men who make monetary gain through the fortune telling of their slave-girl (16.16-24). Exasperated at the girl's repeated shouting concerning his identity, Paul exorcises her spirit of divination, thus depriving her owners of their profits. This leads to the arrest and imprisonment of Paul and Silas under the charge that they are disturbing the city. What follows is a variation on the theme of the prison escape, already encountered previously in the narrative (cf. 5.17-26; 12.1-11). Like Peter before him, Paul is miraculously sprung from jail; he then converts the jailor along with his household. As Roman officials send a message that Paul should be released from custody, Paul makes the dramatic assertion that he and his companion are Roman citizens, who, by virtue of citizenship, should be protected against scourging (16.37). The timing of this announcement strains credulity; had he made it the previous evening, presumably it would have protected him from just such a scourging (16.22-23; cf. 22.24-25, where Paul's assertion of citizenship prevents a scourging that is being prepared for him). The result here is that Roman magistrates turn obsequious, apologizing to the wrongly imprisoned missionary before asking him to leave the city.

The critiques of pagan religious practice in Lystra and in Philippi may be considered a warm-up act for the most well-known Pauline speech in Acts addressed to a Gentile audience concerning Gentile piety, the speech to Athenians in front of the Areopagus (17.22-32). The speech differs radically from those aimed at Jewish synagogue members and their Gentile sympathizers in that it lacks Septuagint quotations, references to Israelite ancestors and (perhaps most strikingly) any substantial discussion of the Christ event, aside from an oblique reference to 'a man' who has been raised by God and who will judge (v. 31). Instead, speaking in the city at the heart of Hellenistic culture, a city famous for philosophy and art, Paul quotes Greek poets, critiques polytheism as born of ignorance once tolerated but no longer excusable (17.30-31), and argues for the one true creator God as the rightful object of piety.

In Corinth (18.1-17), the conflict between Paul and non-believing Jews takes a particular twist that lands him in front of the Roman proconsul, Gallio. While Gallio, unlike Sergius Paulus (13.12), does not convert and is depicted unflatteringly in the end (18.17), he still voices one of the themes of Acts: Christianity's compatibility with Roman rule. After conspiring Jews bring Paul before the tribunal, Gallio refuses to become involved in the dispute, while noting, hypothetically, the terms on which he would have become involved: 'If it were a matter of crime or serious villainy, I would be justified in accepting the complaint of you Jews' (18.14). Through his refusal to hear the charges, because they don't conform to the 'hypothetical' situation he has just established, Gallio witnesses positively toward Christians; Christians are not criminals or villains and, thus, should not be subject to state scrutiny.

Paul's final long term mission site in Acts is the city of Ephesus, where he is said to be based for two years (19.10). The stories of Priscilla and Aquila correcting Apollos in Ephesus (18.24-28) along with Paul's insistence that disciples in Ephesus who have received 'John's baptism' still need

the superior baptism in the name of Jesus (19.1-7) may be read as tantalizing signs of early Christian missions divergent from Paul's own (cf. the
rivalry suggested between Jesus believers loyal to Apollos and those loyal
to Paul in 1 Cor. 10.1-17). Luke here brings these variant missions under
the Pauline umbrella through emphasizing their eventual conformity to the
leadership of Paul and his co-workers. Unfortunately, it is close to impossible to reconstruct these divergent missions in any detail, owing to the
paucity of our sources for them.

Acts 19.11-20 once again takes up the issue of miracles-versus-magic (cf.
8.18-24; 13.6-12) by emphasizing the violent end of those who take part in
the latter practices, while celebrating Paul's wonder-working powers. The
miracles that are credited to Paul here closely resemble stories that will come
to be told of relics of the saints in subsequent centuries: articles of cloth that
Paul himself has touched contain healing powers for those who subsequently
touch these articles. Because such a transfer of power through the touch of
an inanimate object is frequently understood to be a form of 'superstition'
or 'magic' itself, it is here worth remembering the principle long recognized
in comparative religious study concerning the difference between magic and
miracles: miracles are performed by holy people who belong to 'us'; while
magic is a derogatory term for the spiritual practices of 'them'.

Though Paul is said to debate daily in Ephesus, first in the synagogue, and,
eventually, in the lecture hall of Tyrannus, Acts records no speech by Paul
in this city. Indeed, in the episode which is narrated in greatest detail in this
setting, the protest of the silversmiths in the Ephesian theater (19.23-41),
Paul is not even present, much less granted a speaking role. The basis for the
commotion involving the silversmiths, who build shrines to Artemis, is fear
that their business will be imperiled by the popularity of the monotheistic
claims of Christians. (The complaint bears striking resemblance to an observation of the Roman governor of another province in Asia Minor, Pliny the
Younger, in 112 CE, that increasing Christian devotion imperils the sale of
meat related to temple sacrifice; see Pliny's Letter to Trajan concerning the
Christians [*Ep.* 10.96]). In answer to the uproar, the town clerk admonishes
that nothing has been done to justify such a lawless response. He further
invites anyone with a serious charge to pursue it through legal channels. But
at the cessation of the uproar, it is clear that no such channel will be pur-
sued. As Gallio had done in Corinth, so the town clerk in Ephesus suggests
that Christians are doing nothing to merit charges of illegality.

Paul's Final Testament

At the port city of Miletus, on his journey back to Jerusalem, Paul gathers
the elders of the nearby city of Ephesus to deliver a farewell speech, which

closes the missionary section of Acts (20.17-38). Though the book of Acts ends with Paul still living, preaching 'without hindrance' under house arrest in Rome (28.30-31), this speech takes the form of a final testament of one about to die. Paul's accomplishments are reviewed, predictions are made about problems the church will face after his departure (we may presume these problems are faced by Luke as he pens this speech) and allusions to persecution are direct. The speech, along with the ominous prophecy of Agabus concerning Paul's impending martyrdom (21.10-14), suggest to many scholars that Acts was written by an author, and first read by an audience, that knew of Paul's death as a past event.

Paul in Roman Custody, Acts 21.1–28.31

The primary focus of the final eight chapters of Acts is on Paul's defense against charges leveled by Jews as he is under Roman surveillance. The peripatetic missionary, who had circled the northeastern Mediterranean region three times, speaking confidently in synagogues and other public venues of major cities of the empire (Acts 13–20) now enters into narrow spaces of confinement where he will remain until the close of the book. Here Paul, as the falsely accused and innocent missionary, will lay out his defense in a series of speeches: first before hostile crowds in Jerusalem, then before Jewish religious leaders, and, finally, before a series of high-ranking political officials, including the Roman governors, Felix and Festus, and the Jewish client king, Agrippa II. The opportunity to lay his defense before such prominent authorities underscores a special irony in Acts: imprisonment appears not to impede the Pauline mission; on the contrary, it enables him to bear witness to an ever more influential audience, both Roman and Jewish. The heart of his defense will be that Paul has done nothing deserving of punishment and that his mission is merely a pious enactment of the obligations put upon all Jews who understand the promises of their scriptures and the Christ event as the fulfillment of those promises. Thus, though the setting is judicial, the defense lies primarily in the realm of piety, addressing the question of how to interpret the scriptures of Israel properly.

Arrival and Arrest in Jerusalem

The events leading up to his arrest on arrival in Jerusalem (Acts 21.17-36) are some of the most tantalizing and puzzling of all biblical verses for scholars in search of historical details concerning Paul's last days. In Paul's letter to the Romans, which is widely regarded as the final extant letter written by Paul before his death, he speaks of intentions to travel to Spain by way of Rome, but only after first returning to Jerusalem to offer up a collection for the poor of Jerusalem (Rom. 15.18-29). This collection for the poor in Jerusalem is a condition laid upon Paul by the Jerusalem apostles when they approve his mission to the Gentiles (Gal. 2.10). Further, this collection is a central concern that Paul also expresses in 2 Cor. 8 and 9. In Acts' narration of Paul's final visit to Jerusalem, however, the collection—this central Pauline missionary concern—receives no mention.

Instead, Paul is greeted by James and encouraged to demonstrate his zealousness for the law as a means of countering criticism among Jerusalemites that he has been impiously teaching Jews to forsake this law. This criticism raises a further puzzle concerning Acts' relationship to the 'historical Paul', since those with a general knowledge of the Pauline message concerning the law might find James's words here startling. Paul is famous for preaching a 'law-free' gospel, a stance which involves deriding Peter (among others) for adhering to the observance of dietary laws and trumpeting Paul's own refusal to be bound by law in the messianic era (see, especially, Galatians). How could James be depicted here as holding the view that accusations of lawbreaking are unjustified and suggesting that they could be easily rectified?

Careful readers of Paul's own letters and of the accusation relayed by James in Acts might make some progress in resolving this puzzle by noting the distinction here concerning Jews and Gentiles. In James's view, as depicted in Acts, the accusation is that Paul teaches '*Jews*' to forsake the Law of Moses (21.21). This may be considered a false accusation, if it is recognized that Paul's law-free gospel pertains only to Gentiles. That is, if Paul's epistles are read as addressed exclusively to Gentiles and if everything negative Paul says about the law in his epistles pertains only to Gentiles, it is possible to reconcile almost everything in these epistles with James's view here that Paul does not counsel Jews to abandon Moses: (Eisenbaum 2009; Gager 2000).

However much more we would like to know about the collection and about what, precisely, offends those in Jerusalem concerning Paul, Acts will not tell. True to Acts' particular insistence that Christ belief does not entail a departure from Jewish scriptures, Paul is depicted here as agreeing to James's suggestion that he assume the posture of an especially pious law-observer by taking a vow of purification. When he enters the Temple, as part of the fulfillment of that vow, pandemonium ensues. In keeping with the string of false accusations hurled by non-believing Jews against spokespersons for the Jesus movement, Jews 'from Asia' now falsely charge Paul with breaking the law and defiling the Temple (21.27-29). When the mob threatens violence, Roman authorities rush forward to arrest Paul (21.31-33), an action that will remove him from harm from 'the Jews' and keep him in Roman custody from this point to the end of the narrative.

In Acts 22–26, Paul delivers a series of speeches to defend himself to a number of different audiences as he moves through various places of confinement, all the while (and somewhat ironically) seeming to increase in social status and power. Again, owing to Lukan artistry, each of these speeches and the responses they evoke contain particular dramatic and suspenseful details. But for sake of overview, we may pull the following common themes from the events narrated in these chapters:

1. *Paul Has Been Called to Preach to the Gentiles, but He Remains within the Bounds of Judaism as He Carries out his Ministry.* Twice in this section, Paul recounts his conversion from persecutor of, to missionary to, Christians (22.6-21; 26.9-23). Repeatedly, he testifies that he is a Jew, deeply indebted to Jewish (and especially Pharisaic) religious practices and merely quarreling with other Jews about proper interpretation of Jewish practice. At one point, he casts himself on the side of the Pharisees against the Sadducees on the question of the resurrection (23.6). He recounts that his piety involves 'believing everything laid down according to the law or written in the prophets' (24.14-15) and aligns himself with the earnest hope and pious worship of the twelve tribes of Israel (26.6-7).

2. *Non-Believing Jews, Both the Crowds and their Leaders, Are Maniacally Set on Killing Paul.* The crowds intent on killing Paul are only stopped by the Roman tribune's intervention in 21.30-36. After his first defense speech on the Temple steps, they cry for his death again at 22.22-23. The perfidy of 'the Jews' is such that they conspire to the point of taking a vow not to eat or drink until they have murdered him. From the viewpoint of ancient Greco-Roman piety, vowing to undertake a horrendous deed is an act of sacrilege. According to Acts, this sacrilege receives sanction from the highest religious officials in Jerusalem—the chief priests and elders (23.12-15). It would be difficult to imagine how one could denigrate the piety of a social group in terms starker than this. Finally, after Paul is transported to Caesarea for safe keeping, the high priest and elders bring with them the lawyer, Tertullus, to deliver charges of sedition against Paul—charges which, if accepted, would bring the penalty of death and to which 'the Jews' are said to assent (23.1-9).

3. *While Paul is under Roman Custody, Violence and Corruption in the Judicial System Are Not Completely Concealed.* Paul is a prisoner and the violence to which Roman prisoners were subject, gets some airing in these chapters. After dragging him back to the barracks to prevent the Jewish mob from killing him, soldiers prepare him to be flogged and they stop only upon learning of his status as a Roman citizen (22.22-29). The Roman Governor, Felix, keeps Paul in prison for years while hoping to extract money from him and then refuses to

release him as a 'favor' to 'the Jews' (24.26-27). Though Festus, the
successor to Felix, will not only, ultimately, arrange for Paul's appeal
to the emperor, but will also agree that Paul does not deserve death
(26.31), he is, initially, disposed to give Paul up to violent Jews who
would surely kill him, preferring to curry favor with 'the Jews', rather
than to protect one wrongly imprisoned (25.1-9). That Paul is never
released from custody and is subject to the whims of various governors, who look out for their own best interest rather than Paul's,
appears to be both a critique of these officials and Luke's nod to traditions that Paul was killed by Roman authorities. Yet, as we shall see
below, Luke strains mightily against those traditions—to the point of
painting an unbelievable portrait of Roman solicitousness in certain
scenes—in order to underscore that Paul's custody is more for his
protection than for his punishment.

4. *Roman Officials Are Depicted as Surprisingly Absorbed with Paul's
   Particular Circumstance and Do Much to Protect Him from Harm.* A key
   role for Roman authorities, over the course of Paul's final Jerusalem
   visit, is to quell Jewish violence against him. Twice Jews, who are
   attempting to beat Paul to death in front of the Temple, are interrupted by the tribune and his soldiers (21.31-32; 22.22-24). On hearing that Jews are conspiring to ambush Paul as he is shuttled about
   in Jerusalem, the tribune authorizes an escort of incredulous size—
   'two hundred soldiers, seventy horsemen and two hundred spear-
   men'—to transport him to a safer location in Caesarea (23.22-32;
   note also Paul's surprisingly authoritative posture toward a Roman
   centurion while in captivity at 23.17). While he is governor, Felix
   meets frequently for conversation with Paul and Festus carefully lays
   Paul's case before King Agrippa, as if it is of major concern to him
   (25.13-22). After Paul's final defense speech, the king, the governor
   and the king's sister, Berenice, all agree on Paul's innocence (26.31).
   Only because he appeals to Caesar, the prerogative of a Roman citizen, must he be moved from the eastern shores of the Mediterranean
   to the city of Rome.

Many scholars question the historicity of Luke's claim that Paul is a
Roman citizen, in part because Paul himself makes no mention of such status in his own epistles and also because the claim is invoked in Acts always
at moments that increase suspense and move the plot forward, hence seeming to function as a perfect literary device rather than as a historical datum.
Here, the device functions as a means of painting traditions of Paul's death
in Rome in the best light possible. Luke does the best he can to deflect
attention from early Christian traditions that Paul dies at Roman hands;

this Luke does by depicting Paul as following in the footsteps of Jesus as a martyr, going so far to note that, like Jesus, Paul is ready to die '*in Jerusalem*' (21.13) at the hands of perfidious Jews.

The Shipwreck

The story of Paul's journey by sea from Caesarea to Rome (Acts 27.1–28.14) contains a number of literary conventions at home in both ancient epic and novel, including the shipwreck, the hero's brush with a dangerous snake and the hospitality of strangers. The kind reception of Paul by citizens of high standing—in this case, Publius, the 'leading man of the island', (28.7)—underscores a theme repeated throughout the book, as does Paul's ability to heal Publius's father miraculously. Throughout the journey, Paul's heroic oversight guarantees the safety of all travelers; in fact, his assertion of agency is so strong the reader might forget he is actually still in Roman custody. One somewhat remarkable feature of the scene in Malta is that it contains no account of Paul preaching the gospel and, hence, no stories of conversion, or words of condemnation concerning unbelieving Gentiles. The natives are depicted positively as extending hospitality to Paul. As the New Testament scholar, Tatsiong Benny Liew, has noted, this passage might be considered one slender thread of a counter narrative embracing religious pluralism, pushing against the dominant strand of religious exclusivism in the text (Liew 2004).

Arrival in Rome

The relatively lenient conditions of Paul's imprisonment in Rome are pointed out both at his arrival (28.16) and in the final verse of the book, where it is, famously, announced that Paul preaches under house arrest for two years 'without hindrance' (*akōlutōs*, 28.31). The course of events narrated in this last chapter of Acts might puzzle those with knowledge of Paul's letter to the Romans. While the letter to the Romans is addressed to an established community of Christ believers (whom Paul is eager to meet and who have, apparently, heard much about Paul in advance of his visit), Acts mentions Jesus believers in Rome only in passing (28.15) and focuses primarily on his encounters with Jewish leaders in Rome outside of the Christ-believing circle.

The final scene follows a pattern familiar from Paul's missionary journeys; he attempts to persuade Jews that Jesus fulfills the law and the prophets and some believe, while others do not. The book ends ominously for those non-believing Jews, as they are likened to the dull and blind foretold by Isaiah. Their blindness justifies Paul's own prophecy and last recorded words; the salvation of God has now been sent to the Gentiles.

For Further Reading

Byron, Gay
2009   'Ancient Ethiopia and the New Testament: Ethnic (Con)texts and Racialized
        (Sub)texts', in *They Were All Together in One Place? Toward Minority Biblical
        Criticism* (ed. Randall C. Bailey, *et al.*; Atlanta, GA: Society of Biblical
        Literature), pp. 161-90.
Eisenbaum, Pamela
2009   *Paul Was Not a Christian: The Original Message of a Misunderstood Apostle*
        (San Francisco: HarperOne).
Gager, John
2000   *Reinventing Paul* (New York: Oxford University Press, 2000).
Levine, Amy-Jill with Marianne Blickenstaff (ed.)
2004   *A Feminist Companion to the Acts of the Apostles* (London/New York: T. & T.
        Clark International).
Liew, Tat-siong Benny
2004   'Acts', in *The Global Bible Commentary* (ed. Daniel Patte *et al.*; Nashville,
        TN: Abingdon), pp. 419-28.
Pervo, Richard
2009   *Acts: A Commentary* (Hermeneia; Minneapolis, MN: Fortress Press).
Skinner, Matthew
2003   *Locating Paul: Places of Custody as Narrative Settings in Acts 21–28* (Atlanta,
        GA: Society of Biblical Literature).

3

ACTS AND EMPIRE: SECURITY IN ROMAN TERMS

A long-standing question in Acts studies is how best to understand the rhetorical aims of the text vis-à-vis the Roman Empire. A widely held view, asserted most famously by Hans Conzelmann, is that the author of Luke–Acts asserts the compatibility of the Christian faith with loyal subjection to the Roman Empire and attempts to mitigate the tension between the kingdom of God and the reign of Rome. It does so by (1) deferring the *parousia* into the distant future so that its promised upheaval threatens no existing earthly authorities, (2) having Pilate proclaim Jesus' innocence, and (3) by depicting Paul on friendly terms with Roman authorities. A more recent strand of scholarship stresses, to the contrary, that Acts is highly critical of, rather than accommodating towards, empire. These scholars point to strands of the text which hint at a Jesus movement that is countercultural, noting unfavorable portraits of Roman authorities, critique of pagan religiosity and the apostles' uncompromising insistence that Jesus (and, therefore, implicitly, not Caesar) is 'Lord of all'.

This book takes the view that the rhetoric of Acts in terms of empire, while not 'pro-Roman' in any blanket sense, aims to legitimate its social group by highlighting compatibility between its concerns and values and those of the Roman Empire. To be sure, this is not a wholehearted embrace of Romanized culture, as we shall see. But it is a deftly crafted response to those who fear that loyalty to the Jesus movement sets one on a collision course with the cultural and political norms of empire. For the purposes of illustrating how the author of Acts attempts to negotiate a place for his social group within empire, it will be useful to jump ahead a century or more from the time of its composition to consider the purported accusations directed against Christians by a pagan critic.

In the early third century, a Christian apologist named Minucius Felix composed a dialogue between a Christian named Octavius and a Pagan named Caecilius. (It should be immediately noted that, in spite of the modern connotation of the term, a Christian apologist is not one who *apologizes* for the faith, but rather one who defends it [from the Greek *apolegomai*, 'to speak in one's own defense']). Such apologies are literary constructions, not verbatim transcripts of actual historical debates, yet they are quite valuable in providing a general indication of the kinds of critiques leveled against early Christianity and the responses composed by early Christians to address those critiques. Though this particular apology is penned about a hundred years later than the book of Acts, it is revealing, nevertheless, in that it preserves a number of pagan criticisms of the Jesus movement that the book of Acts seems already anxious either to soften or to deflect altogether.

The heart of the critique is aimed at the low social status of early Christians and the clandestine nature of their meetings which, for Romanized observers of the group, was a sure sign of shameful and, potentially, subversive practices. Caecilius, the fictional pagan detractor, complains:

> They have collected from the lowest possible dregs of society the more ignorant fools together with gullible women (readily persuaded, as is their weak sex); they have thus formed a rabble of blasphemous conspirators, who with nocturnal assemblies, periodic fasts, and inhuman feasts seal their pact not with some religious ritual but with desecrating profanation; they are a crowd that furtively lurks in hiding places, shunning the light; they are speechless in public but gabble away in corners ... (Minucius Felix, *Oct.* 8.4 [trans. Clarke]).

He returns, repeatedly, to the problem of furtiveness. Defending his assertion that Christianity must be perverted, he asks:

> Why else should they go to such pains to hide and conceal whatever it is they worship? One is always happy for honorable actions to be made public; crimes are kept secret. Why do they have no altars, no temples, no publicly-known images? Why do they never speak in the open, why do they always assemble in stealth? It must be whatever it is they worship—and suppress—is deserving either of punishment or shame (Minucius Felix, *Oct.* 10.2 [trans. Clarke]).

Caecilius jeers at the object of their veneration, a man subject to the most degrading form of Roman execution, suggesting that the followers of Jesus, who venerate the cross, deserve to be executed on crosses themselves:

> There are also stories about the objects of their veneration: they are said to be a man who was punished with death as a criminal, and the fell wood of his cross, thus providing suitable liturgy for the depraved fiends: they worship what they deserve (Minucius Felix, *Oct.* 9.4 [trans. Clarke]).

He derides them for their disrespect of venerated deities and their withdrawal from society and politics (since Roman religion was both thoroughly public and political, these charges are interrelated):

> They despise our temples as being no more than sepulchers, they spit after our gods, they sneer at our rites, and, fantastic thought it is, our priests

they pity—pitiable themselves; they scorn the purple robes of public office, though they go about in rags themselves (Minucius Felix, *Oct.* 8.4 [trans. Clarke]).

Caecilius indicates some awareness that the deity worshipped by this group is the same god worshipped also by the Jews, a social group for whom he has no love, referring to them as a 'wretched tribe' now captive to the Romans. But he also concedes that even the Jews have a better claim to legitimacy than the Christians, for they, at least, unlike the Christians, worship 'in the open, with temples and altars, with sacrifice and ceremonial' (Minucius Felix, *Octavius* 10.4 [trans. Clarke]).

Again, in spite of the fact that Minucius Felix writes more than a century after Luke, the author of Acts appears to be attuned to virtually identical charges as he writes the book of Acts to reassure his patron, Theophilus. Because Luke seems aware of many of the charges that pagan critics come to hurl against Christians, especially in the second volume of his work, it is often recognized that the book of Acts shares affinities with the early Christian apologists. The Acts narrative may be read as a defense of the faith in narrative form. This chapter will take up these charges, underscored in the writings of Minucius Felix, and examine more closely how Acts might be read as a response to them.

Gullible Women and the Dregs of Society

The author of Luke's Gospel and Acts is sometimes heralded as the 'friend of women' because he includes so many stories of women in the two volumes. But, one who carefully considers the manner in which these women are depicted, particularly in the book of Acts, might come to suspect that 'demonstrating friendliness' toward women is not the overarching rhetorical strategy here. Women are mentioned in the narrative, but, in relation to this narrative, they function peripherally rather than centrally. They seldom speak, and, if they are part of the Jesus movement, they conform to socially accepted roles.

Consider, for example, a problem with 'the widows' in Acts 6.1-6. While many extra-biblical early Christian texts from the second century and beyond suggest that early Christian women, designated as widows, held positions of leadership in the church, in Luke's narrative here they are merely voiceless recipients of charity. There is also material within the New Testament, like 1 Corinthians and the book of Revelation, that point to women's central involvement in early Christian prophecy. While the church historian, Eusebius, hints that the daughters of Philip were recognized leaders in the Christian movement (*Hist. eccl.* 3.31.3-4), Acts provides only the briefest of references to the prophesying daughters of Philip (21.9), declining to give them a speaking part. Lydia, the dealer in purple dye, who welcomes Paul and his companions into her home (16.14-15), appears as respectable as the numerous wealthy women from this region of Asia Minor, who are acknowledged in ancient inscriptions for their public benefactions. She is a recipient of Paul's evangelization, but the depiction is passive; the text stresses that the Lord opened her heart to receive Paul's words. Unlike Euodia and Syntyche, the women known from Paul's letter to the Philippians (4.2), Lydia seems neither to have shared in theological leadership nor to have formulated opinions of her own. It is also the case that, though she is the sole actor in her household, her entire household is said to have been baptized after she embraces Paul's message, thereby raising the thorny issues of agency and will in household baptisms (though the narrative is silent on the matter, household baptisms would, presumably, have involved forced conversions).

In the Acts narrative, the leadership of the early Christian movement is overwhelmingly male. This is explicitly underscored through repeated use of the gender specific Greek word *anēr* ('male') over the more inclusive *anthrōpos* ('human', less frequently used of a 'man' specifically). (Biblical scholar, Mary Rose D'Angelo [2002], notes that, while the Gospel of Mark employs *anthrōpos* most frequently and *anēr* in only 4 instances, the Third Gospel uses *anēr* some 27 times and Acts employs the term around 50 times.) In Peter's Pentecost speech for example, he addresses 'Men (*andres*), Judeans' (2.14), 'Men (*andres*), Israelites' (2.22); 'Men (*andres*), brothers' (2.29). Acts stresses the privileged authority granted to the 'the Twelve' and insists that maleness is a required quality for the candidate chosen to replace Judas among the twelve (1.21-22; note that this tradition of the primacy of the Twelve stands in marked contradiction to the Gospel of John, where leadership is not only much more fluid, but also, apparently, includes the sisters Mary and Martha of Bethany). The seven appointed to serve at table as a means of resolving the controversy over the widows in Acts 6.1-6 are also all men.

Acts' rhetorical concern to emphasize the manliness of the Jesus movement is particularly apparent if one considers not only what is said, but also what is left out of Luke's story of women in early Christianity. In Paul's epistles, we come across a number of women, named and unnamed, who seem to have assumed a variety of leadership roles among the emerging assembly (*ekklēsia*). Romans 16 is a veritable treasure trove of such women, with Phoebe (sister, minister, president), Prisca (co-worker for whom Paul gives thanks) and Junia (apostle) receiving the most interesting leadership titles, but others are also included in the naming. In Phil. 4.2, as noted above, Syntyche and Euodia are mentioned as Paul's co-workers in that city; 1 Corinthians, while naming only a few women, suggests that the role of women in communal prayer and prophesy is one of the largest issues of contention between Paul and the Corinthian assembly (see especially 1 Cor. 7; 11.2-16; 14.33b-36). The Gospels, likewise, tell of numerous named and unnamed women in the Jesus movement. Perhaps the most notable woman of all within the Jesus movement is Mary Magdalene, who holds a prominent role as witness to the crucifixion and resurrection in canonical Gospel traditions, a role that is also elaborated and magnified in the numerous extra-biblical writings concerning her.

In contrast, aside from the references to Prisca/Priscilla, introduced as 'the wife of Aquila' as part of the narrative plot in Acts 18 (vv. 2, 18, 26), suggestions of women's leadership in the movement are, at best, fleeting. Particularly puzzling, given the numerous extra-biblical traditions of Mary Magdalene's prominence among the disciples after Jesus' departure, is Acts' absolute silence concerning this post-resurrection witness and companion of Jesus (the closest we get is a reference to the presence of 'certain women' in the company of the Twelve and Jesus' brothers in the upper room awaiting the promised descent of the Holy Spirit, in 2.14). In short, the gullible women that populate the Christian movement in Caecilius's view are removed from Acts' more orderly account.

As to the question of where the 'dregs of society', both men and women, fit in the Acts narrative, a primary answer is that they are objects of charity. The image of Peter and John healing a man lame from birth in Acts 3.1-10 resonates with stories told in the Third Gospel of Jesus' ministry to the poor and outcast. Peter performs such acts of mercy among the socially marginalized again in Acts 9.32-42; he heals a paralyzed man, who had been bedridden for years, and then raises a widow, devoted to charitable acts, from the dead. But while there are gestures toward charitable ministries among the lowly in Acts, the central concern in Acts is not with the very lowest ranks of the social ladder; often it is pointed toward the very highest rungs.

We have already spoken of Lydia, the dealer in purple dye in Acts 16, who receives Paul's message and has her household converted as a result. As a merchant trading in a luxury commodity, she is marked out as having some measure of wealth. Much higher up on the social ladder than Lydia are: the court official of the Ethiopian queen converted by Philip in Acts 9; the Roman proconsul (governor by Roman senatorial appointment!) of Cyprus, Sergius Paulus, who is converted by Paul; the Asiarchs (highly placed governmental officials in the Greek East) who look after Paul's welfare in Ephesus (19.30-31); and the Roman centurions who aid and protect Paul during his trip to Rome (27.3, 43). One of the most important conversion stories in Acts, to which an entire chapter is devoted, concerns Cornelius (Acts 10). As noted in a previous chapter, the scene is pivotal in establishing the principle of Gentile inclusion, without dietary restrictions or other 'burdens' of the Jewish Law, among followers of the Way. The length of the chapter and the importance of its resolution with respect to the inclusion of Gentiles suggest to many scholars that Cornelius should be understood as the ideal type of a Christian convert. Notably, Cornelius is no ordinary Gentile, but rather a centurion, a highly placed officer of the Italian cohort.

Even in scenes where the characters are not singled out as high-standing, the reader's attention is often directed upward rather than downward. Consider the mantic slave girl in 16.16-21, who annoys Paul by announcing his status as servant of the Most High God. Paul exorcises the spirit of her prophecy, but this healing does not result in the inclusion of this exploited slave girl into the community of Christians, instead, she drops from the scene after her role as narrative prop in the story is over (the exorcism prompts the charges that land Paul and Silas in jail). This story is followed by another that focuses on affirming the established order, rather than meeting the needs of the oppressed. The miraculous earthquake, which enables Paul and Silas to spring from jail (16.25-40), loosens not just their chains, but those of all the prisoners with whom they share captivity. This release causes the jailor to become despondent; he is ready to commit suicide at the thought that a prison break has occurred on his watch. Paul saves the jailor from this fate by reassuring him that no one has escaped. The narrative then shifts to the jailor's conversion, without further mention of the prisoners and whether or not they remain free or returned willingly to their holding places. This lack of interest in the fate of the rest of the prisoners suggests some dissonance between this story and the inaugural sermon of Jesus in the Third Gospel, where a core element of Jesus' ministry is identified as 'proclaiming release to the captives' (Lk. 4.18).

The most direct means by which Acts refutes the charge that Christians are drawn from the dregs of society is to depict the leaders of the movement speaking at length with rhetorical finesse. Since education in oratorical performance was a defining component of elite male socialization in the Greco-Roman world—what biblical scholar, Todd Penner, has identified as 'civilizing discourse'—those who possess it simply could not come from the lowest ranks of society. The depiction of Christian leaders as skilled orators is not only a means of elevating their status in answer to the charge 'they are of the lowest classes', as we consider below, it also serves to rebut the concomitant charge that Christians are secretive, gathering only in the dark.

Jabbering in Corners

If all of the public speeches contained in Acts were signified in red (on the model of the red letter versions of the Bible which feature Jesus' words in this way), Acts would be a very red text. Speeches occupy such a prominent place in the book of Acts, in comparison to other ancient histories, biographies and novels, that some scholars have argued that the speeches contain the primary message of Acts and that the shorter bits of narrative between the speeches function only to provide context for them. One effect of these speeches is to give the lie to any accusation from outsiders that early Christians 'lurk in hiding places' or 'gabble away in corners'. Far from being a secret society of gabblers (and Roman officials regarded anything secret as potentially seditious and sedition the likely path for those without proper rhetorical/civilizing education), the spokespersons for the movement speak openly and boldly in public settings with rhetorical finesse, thereby embodying Greco-Roman ideals of citizenship. (Note that in his defense before the Roman Governor, Festus, Paul explicitly emphasizes that the things of this movement were 'not done in a corner'; see Malherbe [1985-86].)

In broad terms, we can classify the speeches of Acts into two categories: First, as part of public deliberation over some aspect of the group's polity, whether that deliberation is set within the group (e.g. see Acts 15) or as an address to prospective converts (e.g. see 13.16-41); second, as eloquent defense against spurious charges of unworthy opponents (e.g. see 7.2-53; 26.2-23). These two categories of public speech, persuasion and defense, were regarded as pillars of the rhetorical education upon which civic life in the Roman world was predicated. Thus, through their eloquent speech, Peter, James, Stephen and, especially, Paul are depicted as exemplary models of citizenship.

Worshiping the Crucified

Not unsurprisingly, pagan skeptics scorned the Christian practice of venerating a crucified man as a god, since crucifixion was the punishment that the Roman Empire reserved for the most degraded lot of criminals. Luke does not deny that Jesus was both crucified and yet proclaimed, among Christians, as Lord and God, but a redactional trend to diminish certain aspects of the tradition concerning Jesus as *crucified* Lord, which begins in the Third Gospel, is elaborated at even greater length in the book of Acts.

The Third Gospel includes the story of Jesus meeting the punishment of crucifixion, but also modifies the tradition for the purposes of (1) diminishing Roman involvement in that crucifixion, (2) heightening Jewish culpability for the death, and (3) stressing the innocence and nobility of Jesus as he undergoes this unjust fate. This Gospel is distinct among the canonical Gospels for putting into Pontius Pilate's mouth the threefold proclamation that Jesus, as an innocent man, does not deserve to be crucified (23.4, 14-15, 22). Thus, Luke makes the point that while Jesus was indeed crucified, it was an unjust punishment, as even the highest Roman provincial authority in Judea knew full well. Moreover, Luke's passion makes several connections between the death of Jesus and that of Socrates, the paradigm for the unjustly killed wise man in Greek and Roman tradition, once again answering the scorn associated with crucifixion with the response that Jesus suffered execution wrongly (and, like Socrates, nobly). Finally, the Third Gospel heightens the role of Jewish agency in demanding Jesus' death, thereby accounting for the crucifixion as owing, primarily, not to the disciplinary machinery of the Roman Empire, but rather to Jewish depravity.

In Acts, the innocence of Jesus is also a given and the blame for his death is placed even more firmly upon 'the Jews' as chief executioners. Instances of blame for Jesus' death being attached solely to Jews, Judeans, Israelites and/ or Jerusalemites, without mention of Roman involvement, include 2.22-23, 36; 3.12-15a; 4.10; 5.30; 7.51-52; 10.39 and 13.27-28. In only one instance, at 4.27-28, are both Roman/Gentile and Jewish authorities implicated for Jesus' death ('For in this city, in fact, both Herod and Pontius Pilate, with the Gentiles and the peoples of Israel, gathered together against your holy servant Jesus, whom you anointed, to do whatever your hand and your plan had predestined to take place'). While Acts repeatedly stresses the unjustness of the execution, along with Jewish culpability for that execution, it is not often explicit about the manner of the execution. Acts never uses the word 'cross' as a substantive. Only twice does Acts employ the verb 'to crucify' (2.36; 4.10) and, in both cases, Jews are the agents of crucifixion. Euphemisms for the death, such as 'handed over', are preferred. In two mentions of Jesus' death, 'the Jews' are said to have carried out the execution by 'hanging him on a tree' (5.30; 10.39; cf. 13.29), thus, conjuring up a Jewish lynching rather than a Roman state punishment.

It is also the case that Acts stresses the resurrection and ultimate vindication of Jesus much more than the crucifixion itself. The narrative, which begins with the ascension of Jesus into the heavens, stresses this elevation as a key aspect of Jesus' nature (e.g. see 7.56; 13.33-37; 17.31); in Paul's speech in Athens to the Council of the Areopagus, he withholds any mention of Jesus at all until the climax of his speech, where it is somewhat cryptically noted that God will judge the world in righteousness 'by a man whom he has appointed, and of this he has given assurance to all by raising him from the dead' (17.31b). Paul, in his defense speeches during legal proceedings against him, also highlights that his proclamation concerned belief in resurrection, rather than any association with a crucified man, as the source of the false accusations against him (23.6; 24.15, 21; 26.6-8).

In short, Acts does not deny the crucifixion of Jesus, but it does not dwell on it. This text's minimization of the crucifixion comes into stark relief when it is contrasted with the centrality of the cross in Paul's reflections on his ministry in his epistles. In 1 Corinthians, Paul asserts his conscious decision to reduce the message of his gospel to nothing but Christ crucified. ('For Jews demand signs and Greeks desire wisdom, but we proclaim Christ crucified', 1 Cor. 1.22-23; 'When I came to you, brothers and sisters, I did not come proclaiming the mystery of God to you in lofty words or wisdom. For I decided to know nothing among you except Jesus Christ, and him crucified', 1 Cor. 2.1-2). Paul asserts here that such proclamation is regarded as 'foolishness' to the Gentiles. A hostile outsider, such as Caecilius, would certainly concur, as Luke himself seems aware. In contrast to Paul , who, in his letters, embraces this 'foolishness', Luke prefers to direct the attention of his readers elsewhere.

Spitting at the Gods and Scorning Public Robes

From the perspective of a hostile outsider, Christians were regarded as atheists and sociopaths and scorned for neither engaging in the worship of the gods of the cities in which they resided nor assuming civic duties in which such worship would have played an integral part. Here is a point where Luke is most uncompromising in constructing his narrative, for he does not overtly refute the charge that Christians do not participate in civic/pagan cultic practices. Christians, in his narrative, are never depicted as engaging in the worship of pagan deities or participating in the cult of the Roman Emperor. Once converted, they are not elected to city councils or to pagan priesthoods in any of the cities in which they live or to which they travel. Luke's rhetorical strategy here is not to deny the charge, but to soften the social and political effects of Christian non-participation in polytheistic practices.

The dramatic episode in Ephesus concerning the silversmiths and their claims on Artemis, depicted in Acts 19, provides one illustration of this rhetorical strategy. The goddess Artemis was widely known in the ancient Mediterranean world as the chief deity of Ephesus. The temple to her in that city, with more than 120 huge columns gilded in silver and gold and adorned with the finest of paintings and sculpture, was regarded as one of the seven wonders of the ancient world. Luke is cognizant of the fame of the Ephesian Artemis, acknowledging the city's privileged status as *neokoros*—or temple guardian (19.35). He draws on this knowledge to construct a scene in which the clash of loyalties to their respective deities leads to a perilous situation for Paul and his companions.

The episode begins with an accusation by Demetrius, an Ephesian silversmith who earns a living crafting Artemis shrines, that Paul and his companions deny the value of images of the gods and also threaten the majestic standing of Artemis in all of Asia. A commotion ensues, which threatens to degenerate into a serious riot. But it is diffused by the town clerk, who provides the following reassurance at the culmination of the scene: '[T]hese men here ... are neither temple robbers nor blasphemers of our goddess' (19.37). Thus, the reassurance is conveyed: on the one hand, Paul and his companions surely do not drum up any business for the silversmiths constructing shrines, for they are non-participatory, as Caecilius knows, but on the other hand, they are not so impiously hostile that they would 'spit on the gods', as Caecilius accuses. They are, rather, defended by the town clerk as those 'who do not blaspheme' the great Ephesian goddess.

Another way that Luke softens the charge of anti-social, anti-religious behavior on the part of Christians, without going so far as to depict them as engaged in Greco-Roman cultic practice, is to assert that Paul is on friendly terms with civic/religious officials of the highest social standing in the city, namely, the Asiarchs of Ephesus (19.31). R.A. Kearsley has recently compiled inscriptional evidence concerning the roles of Asiarchs to demonstrate that they were civic rather than provincial officials (an older view had held that Asiarchs were provincial officers of the emperor cult). Civic responsibilities evidenced in these inscriptions include civic building projects, civic temple duties, presiding over civic games and festivals and, in the second century, providing gladiator combats and animal hunts (Kearsley 1994). The scorn for Christian anti-social, anti-religious behavior is answered in Acts with the counter narrative that Christians are befriended and protected by highly-placed officials. While these officials are themselves thoroughly immersed in 'pagan' civic/religious practices, they have no apparent qualms with Christian non-participation. Indeed, their loyalty to the Christians extends so far that they are willing to defend them from detractors.

Finally, consider the rhetorical strategy of 'silence', employed in the story of Cornelius (Acts 10), concerning the implications of conversion to Christianity for those involved in governmental responsibilities. After the conversion of this centurion, the universal lordship of Jesus is proclaimed by Peter (10.36). The fact that this convert is a ranking member of the Roman military stationed in Caesarea, a city founded in honor of Caesar Augustus, suggests that Cornelius, undoubtedly, knows of a 'rival lord' to whom he bears obligations, namely, Lord Caesar. But whether or not Cornelius feels mixed loyalties to both Jesus *and* Caesar, whether he feels obligated to resign from his military leadership role owing to his conversion or whether he is pressured to remain silent concerning his loyalty to his new lord, are simply questions that Acts does not entertain in the text. Acts celebrates the conversion of a Roman centurion, but, aside from reassuring readers that he can eat at the same table with Jewish Jesus believers, Luke raises no issues about the social and political consequences such a convert would face.

Worse than the 'Wretched Tribe' of the Jews

The question of Acts and the Jews will require its own chapter, owing to the complexity and weight of this issue. Here I note only that Acts steers a fine line on the question, wanting to affirm that any positive cultural value associated with Israelite heritage may be claimed by Christians, who are the true heirs of God's promises to Israel. Any negative association that accrues to the Jews, particularly as instigators of revolts against Roman rule, functions to drive a wedge between followers of the Way and Jews who are non-believers. As we shall see in more detail in the next chapter, the latter are depicted in stark colors as being just as seditious, disorderly and prone to irrational violence as elite Romans such as Tacitus assume them to be. As typical of a minority group that is seeking a safe place under empire, Luke attempts to secure a place for his own people by targeting another minority group as unworthy of such security.

Conclusion

Only in the second century were Christians gaining visibility as a social group distinct enough from Jews, at least in some quarters, to attract the attention and suspicion of learned Gentile critics as a new religious cult (this is not to say that in the early second century *all* Jesus believers everywhere were distinctly separate from other Jews; e.g. see ancient literature traditionally classified under the rubric of 'Jewish Christianity', along with the burgeoning secondary scholarship on the question). In a society in which only established ancient religious practices were valued, new religious cults were derided as superstitions. In response to these criticisms, learned Christians penned a number of apologetic treatises to refute these charges (in addition to the *Octavius* of Minucius Felix, see, for example, the well-known apologies of Justin Martyr and Tertullian, along with Origen's *Against Celsus*).

One reason for the resurgence of interest in dating Acts to the second century is the fact that this text also seems cognizant of the many charges levied against Christians by their despisers beginning in the second century. The rhetorical strategy employed by the author of Acts in the face of criticism is a mix of affirming some of these charges while attempting to soften their effects and denying other accusations altogether. Christians are not polytheists and they reverence neither the emperor nor any idol, but Acts insists that this does not make them sociopaths. Instead, leading civic officials, who do engage in such religious practices, are depicted as friendly toward Christian leaders, apparently unbothered with their distinctive and intolerant religious claims. Acts does not deny that the Jesus whom Christians worship was crucified, but the cross and the crucifixion do not supply central meaning to the Acts text, as they do in the Pauline epistles; focus, instead, is on the resurrection, the triumphant ascension, the judgment to come and the fact that the fault for Jesus' execution lies with "the Jews." The issue of the composition of early Christian communities and the potentially subversive nature of the movement are charges Luke refutes most directly. He does this with two rhetorical strategies. On the one hand, he tells a 'manly story' of the Christian movement in which elite male leaders of the Way engage in skilled oratorical displays, while women and "the dregs" are depicted as marginal to the movement's success; on the other hand, he shows that charges of subversion raised against Christians are baseless.

As already noted in a previous chapter, Acts' preoccupation with refuting charges that followers of the Way were, indeed, civic troublemakers does suggest that Luke knows a different story of the early Christians, one in which the actions of Jesus believers were in some ways counter-cultural and politically subversive. We will explore that possibility in greater depth in our concluding chapter on the Pentecost and the issue of early Christian multivocity. In the chapter immediately following this one, we turn to face a thorny issue that has been mentioned repeatedly in this guide and which merits its own chapter: the question of Acts and the Jews.

For Further Reading

Conzelmann, Hans
1961   *Theology of St Luke* (New York: Harper & Row).
D'Angelo, Mary Rose
2002   'The ANHP Question in Luke–Acts: Imperial Masculinity and the Deployment of Women in the Early Second Century', in *A Feminist Companion to Luke* (ed. Amy-Jill Levine; Sheffield: Sheffield Academic Press), pp. 44-69.
Esler, Philip
1987   *Community and Gospel in Luke-Acts: The Social and Political Motivations of Lucan Theology* (Cambridge: Cambridge University Press).
Kearsley, R.A.
1985-86 'The Asiarchs', in *The Book of Acts in Its Graeco-Roman Setting* (ed. David W.J. Gill and Conrad Gempf; Grand Rapids, MI: Eerdmans), pp. 363-76.

Malherbe, Abraham
1985-86 '"Not in a Corner": Early Christian Apologetic in Acts 26.26', *SecCent* 5:
    pp. 193-210.
Matthews, Shelly
2010 'Situating Acts', in *Perfect Martyr: The Stoning of Stephen and the Construction
    of Christian Identity* (New York: Oxford University Press), pp. 27-51.
Penner, Todd
2007 'Civilizing Discourse: Acts, Declamation, and the Rhetoric of the Polis', in
    Contextualizing Acts: Lukan Narrative and Greco-Roman Discourse (ed. Todd
    Penner and Caroline Vander Stichele; Leiden: Brill), pp. 65-104.
Rowe, C. Kavin
2009 *World Upside Down: Reading Acts in the Graeco-Roman Age* (Oxford: Oxford
    University Press).

4

ACTS ON JEWS AND JUDAISM:
VIOLENCE 'TURNED INWARD' UNDER EMPIRE

The book of Acts has long been regarded as articulating an early form of Christian supersessionism, the belief that Israel forfeited its standing as the people of God through its rejection of Jesus and that this favored status then transferred to the believing Gentiles/Christians, who accepted Jesus as messiah and true fulfillment of the Jewish scriptures. This appears to be the force of Paul's closing words at the end of Acts. Here he rebukes the Jewish community in Rome for their blindness by quoting a harsh passage from the prophet Isaiah. He closes the quote with the ominous words: 'Let it be known to you then that this salvation of God has been sent to the Gentiles; they will listen' (28.28; cf. 13.46 and 18.6 to see the threefold pattern in Acts of Paul's rebuke of Jews and turn to Gentiles).

In recent decades, Christian scholars have become more sensitive to the long history of Christian anti-Judaism linked to such notions of Christian supersession. They have sought to establish rapprochement between Christians and Jews by arguing that Christianity, in its earliest forms, was not so anti-Jewish after all (see, for example, Brawley, 1987; Slingerland, 1986; Tiede 1993).

By far the most prevalent approach to defending the author of Acts from the charge of anti-Judaism is to insist that, because Acts is written before Christianity has become a separate religion, Acts itself presents a *Jewish* perspective. In this line of thinking, the quarrel between the author of Acts and other Jews should be read as an intramural debate. Any angry words hurled against non-believing Jews should be understood as consistent with the harsh judgments delivered by biblical prophets to their own people. Read in this way, the book of Acts stands in continuity with the books of Isaiah and Jeremiah, which also contain excoriating judgment against a recalcitrant people. While its message concerning non-believing Jews might be harsh, this message is delivered in the ultimate hope that it might lead to changed behavior, repentant hearts and a renewed commitment to the covenant. Since Paul's quotation from the biblical prophet Isaiah promises healing to *everyone* who turns, including any Jews who become believers in Christ, the book's final word is really one of hope for Jewish repentance and salvation.

It is further noted that, far from rejecting Judaism, Acts actually embraces it by stressing the Jewish credentials of its leaders and the importance of Jewish institutions, including the Temple and the scriptures. Paul's own careful observance of Jewish law is underscored through his speeches and actions, including a demonstration of his willingness to take a vow as proof of his piety when others call his piety into question (21.23-26). The report of James that 'myriads' of Jews have come to confess Christ is celebrated on Paul's return to Jerusalem (21.20). Even the Pharisees, those most careful observers of Jewish law, can be depicted in surprisingly positive ways in this text (5.34-39; 23.6-9).

A third line of argument in defending Acts from the charge of anti-Judaism begins with the concession that Acts does, indeed, contain polemic against Jews. But it then moves to qualify that polemic by insisting that the angry words toward, and critical depictions of, non-believing Jews are not blanket condemnations. Rather than being directed against all non-believing Jews everywhere, the polemic targets only a certain kind of Jew: either the Jewish leadership/establishment or only those Jews who live specifically in the city of Jerusalem or the land of Judea. That is, the critique hinges on the question of leadership office or geographic coordinates; it is local and specific rather than global.

In what follows, each of these recent proposals for downplaying the anti-Jewish nature of rhetorical markers in Acts will be called into question and a version of the traditional view of Acts' anti-Judaism affirmed. While sympathizing with the larger goal of working toward rapprochement among Jews and Christians, I myself am not of the view that exculpating the author of Acts from charges of anti-Judaism is the best way forward. Such an approach must overlook obvious rhetorical strategies employed by Luke to denigrate virtually all Jews who do not confess Jesus as Christ. It further ignores several textual indications that the author of Acts, writing in the early second century, has some awareness that his social group no longer stands entirely within the walls of Judaism, but is in the process of forming new social allegiances. After laying out my understanding of how Acts maps these distinctions, I will conclude with some ways of thinking through the problem of Acts and anti-Judaism without denying that the problem exists.

The Nature of Intramural Polemic

It is true that Jewish scriptures play a central role in Acts' condemnation of non-believing Jews. Luke's citations from the prophets include words of condemnation from both Isaiah and Jeremiah, and yes, these prophets cast some notoriously polemical words against their people as a means of accounting for national catastrophe in terms of corporate sin. (For citations from prophets active at the times of the destructions of the First and the Second Temples which excoriate the people in particularly harsh language, see especially Tiede 1999.) Furthermore, as with the biblical prophets, a primary message of the speeches in Acts directed toward Jews is the need for repentance. Finally, it should be noted that while Luke knows that the word 'Christian' has been applied to members of his social group, he does not himself employ the term as the proper name of the social group the development of which he narrates. Paul emphatically identifies himself as a Jew, but never as a Christian. Here, as in other cases, Luke seems more concerned to communicate that followers of the Way are 'true Jews', rather than members of some alternate group that outsiders might regard as a splinter group or sect. That Luke employs biblical prophecy, that he calls (as a good prophet should) for the repentance of the people and that he does not use the word 'Christian' as it later comes to be used to designate a religion distinct from Judaism, are arguments marshaled to make the case that Luke is engaged in intramural polemic, rather than polemic from outside the walls.

The problem with seeing Luke as inside of the walls of the Jewish community turns on the fact that he has introduced a new variable into the equation as he asserts what is required to receive repentance and salvation. In classical biblical prophecy, repentance requires a turning back to what has been established as the good. A typical formulation of such a call requires reminding what the law designates as proper and just behavior and calling people, who have departed from those laws, back to proper observance. Consider, for instance, the polemic of Amos 2.8 against those who have unjustly used 'garments taken in pledge'. The accusation here is that such persons have violated pre-existing divine laws concerning proper use of collateral secured from the poor (preserved in the Torah: Exod. 22.26-27 and Deut. 24.17). From the prophet's point of view, a proper response from those hearing this condemnation would be repentance, signified by a turn to observance of these pre-established laws.

In contrast, the call for repentance in Acts requires turning to something new, rather than to something pre-established, namely, turning to the confession that Jesus is the messiah who was prophesied in scriptures. In this sense, calls for 'repentance' among the Jews in Acts are really calls to conversion to Christ belief. Luke may be holding out hope for the Jews of Rome by putting into Paul's mouth, at the close of Acts, a quotation from Isaiah concerning how those who are blinded might turn and be healed. But his hope here is for a turn to the proclamation of Jesus as messiah.

Furthermore, while Acts might not employ the categories 'Jew' and 'Christian' in the way that they will come to be employed to distinguish two separate religions, Luke is grasping toward those categories by making another near absolute divide in his narrative: on the one hand, there are those Jews who confess Christ and, thus, might be saved; on the other, there are Jews who do not and, thus, 'have judged themselves to be unworthy of eternal life' (13.14). In some instances this distinction is made through a very awkward use of the category 'Jew', as if Luke is straining for another word to categorize them that is just out of his reach. See, for instance, the narrative where Apollos is cast as a Jew—*Ioudaios tis Apollōs*—who is noted for powerfully and publically 'refuting the Jews' through his demonstrations that Jesus is the Christ (18.24-28). It could be said that Acts is a book in which individual Jews—Stephen, Apollos, Peter and, quintessentially, Paul—'vehemently refute the Jews' through these demonstrations concerning the Christ.

To be sure, the walls that will come to separate Christians from Jews altogether have not been firmly established in Luke's time (and some would argue that they have always been porous, even beyond the fourth-century establishment of Christian orthodoxy and rabbinic Judaism), but Luke is in the process of constructing a new set of boundaries and borderlines, with his group on one side and non-believing Jews on the other.

We now turn to the question of whether Luke's embrace of Jews who do confess Christ, as well as his embrace of Jewish institutions and practices, would enable us to argue that Luke is not anti-Jewish. Here we must consider Luke's rhetorical strategies concerning Jews in view of the larger context of the Roman Empire in which he writes.

Roman Perspectives on Jews and Judaism

We cannot fully understand relations inscribed between non-believing Jews and followers of the Way, or Christians, in Acts without taking a third party into consideration: Roman and Romanized viewers of foreign religious practices, in general, and of Jewish practices, in particular. It takes no great research skills to find ancient Roman literary works which denigrate Jews. Both Cicero and Seneca regard Jewish practices as no more than barbaric superstition. A fragment from Petronius's *Satryica* singles out both the practice of circumcision and abstention from pork for ridicule ('The Jew may worship his pig-god and clamor in the ears of high heaven, but unless he also cuts back his foreskin with the knife, he shall go forth from the people and emigrate to Greek cities, and shall not tremble at the fasts of Sabbath imposed by the law'; Petronius, Fragment 37 LCL [trans. Heseltine]). Jews are often lumped together with devotees of Isis, Dionysos and Cybele as practitioners of the strange and exotic religions from the east that pollute the Roman capital and captivate gullible women (e.g. see the sixth satire of Juvenal). The early second-century historian, Tacitus, asserts that the

Jews engage in practices diametrically opposed to Roman/human norms: '[Moses] ... introduced new religious practices, opposed to those of all other religions. The Jews regard as profane all that we hold sacred; on the other hand, they permit all that we abhor' (*Hist.* 5.4 LCL [trans. Moore]). Writing between the first Jewish-Roman war in Judea (66–70 CE) and the second Jewish-Roman war in the provinces (115–117 CE), Tacitus levels the harsh verdict that Jerusalem is a magnet attracting the 'vast rabble' ejected from other cities and that Jews are perpetually engaged in sedition (*Histories* 5.12).

This portrait of Jews as suspiciously foreign, misanthropic and seditious, however, is only one side of the coin, for other historical sources are more favorable, suggesting begrudging admiration for, and sometimes even enthusiastic emulation of, Jewish practices. It is no longer accepted by scholars, as it once was, that Jews had a special and long-standing legal 'charter' guaranteeing universal privileges throughout the Roman Empire. Yet, the Jewish historian, Josephus, does provide a series of political decrees, in his *Antiquities*, suggesting Roman administrative tolerance of Jews (however haphazard and tenuous). A handful of literary sources also suggests that Judaism found converts, or at least sympathizers, among those of high social standing in Rome. The writings of Hellenistic Jews, such as Philo and Josephus, concur with the archeological evidence in the Greek East in suggesting integration of Jews into city life in these regions.

Explanation for this tolerance in the Roman period can be found in the fact that Romans placed enormous value on the antiquity of their origins and polity and, thus, could respect other cultures which also claimed origins in the long distant past and engaged in polities that were perceived to be stable over time. From the perspective of a ruling power that valued antiquity as a sign of stability, Jews could be regarded as having a measure of cultural capital, owing to the ancientness of their scriptures, the nobility of Moses their lawgiver, the wisdom of their prophets and the long-standing nature of their customs and practices.

To be sure, this measure of cultural capital was slight and held only tenuously, particularly so after the Roman war with Judea (66–70 CE) and the continued violent clashes between Jews and other residents of the provinces that spiked in the years 115–117 CE. Here it may be helpful to remember the distinction made by 'the pagan' Caecilius in Minucius Felix's third-century dialogue discussed in the previous chapter. On the one hand, this critic of Christianity disparages the Jews, regarding them as a 'wretched tribe' now properly captive to Roman overlords. But signs of a second opposing sentiment are also at work when he, at least, recognizes that Jews (unlike the Christians, in his view) are engaged in public, legitimate and recognizable forms of pious practice.

Enter the author of Acts, whose concern is to legitimize Paul's mission to the Gentiles, which is focused geographically in the Aegean basin, clustered in major Romanized cities, such as Corinth, Thessalonica, Philippi and Ephesus. The churches associated with Paul in this region in the second century were largely, if not exclusively, Gentile. While, on the one hand, Jewish scriptures would have been central to these communities and members of these churches claimed identity within 'Israel', on the other hand, from the perspective of an observing outsider, the communities did not look to be particularly Jewish. Composed primarily of Gentiles, not observing the well-known Jewish customs of circumcision and abstention from pork and worshiping an executed criminal as a god, these Christians would be subject to accusations of adhering to a new religion and a suspiciously subversive one at that.

It is with a view to this triangular relationship affecting Romans, Jews and Christians that Acts is crafted. The rhetorical strategy is twofold. First, Acts argues that Israelite scriptures reach their end point in confession of Jesus as the promised messiah. Those who make this confession, whether Jew or Gentile, are truly Israel. Inherent in this claim is the assumption of the positive cultural capital accrued by Jews due to their antiquity. Second, Acts deflects the charge that Christians are superstitious and seditious onto Jews who do not confess Jesus as messiah, a strategy wielded both as an assertion of Christian innocence and to create a clear distinction between Luke's group and non-believing Jews. Acts' message concerning the latter is that these non-believing Jews are just as violent and socially degenerate as the most negative Roman perceptions made them out to be. They are, indeed, as the Roman historian, Tacitus, would say, engaged in perpetual sedition. This rhetorical strategy typifies what those who study imperial power call the common phenomenon of 'violence turned inward'—one minority group under empire struggling to gain a foothold with those in power by denigrating another similarly placed colonized group. Acts' message that its own group is 'truly Israel' leads to its embrace of certain aspects of Judaism, a topic to which we now turn.

Acts' Love of 'Things Jewish'

We begin here with a quick overview of the ways in which the author of Acts stresses the Jewish roots of the movement the unfolding of which he traces.

Centrality of Jerusalem and the Jerusalem Temple

Jerusalem looms large in the Gospel of Luke. The opening scene of the Gospel concerns the priest Zechariah and his Temple duties in Jerusalem;

once Jesus 'sets his face toward Jerusalem' in Lk. 9.51, his travels are plotted in a straight geographical line from Galilee to Jerusalem; in contrast to the rest of the canonical Gospels, Luke ends with disciples worshiping in the Jerusalem Temple after having seen the resurrected Jesus (Lk. 24.52-53), rather than traveling to Galilee (cf. Mk. 16.7; Jn. 21). Acts also begins in Jerusalem, where the disciples are instructed to wait for the descent of the Holy Spirit (1.4). The disciples pray in the Jerusalem Temple and teach on the Temple steps. Though a scattering from Jerusalem takes place owing to persecution at the death of Stephen, the city crops up repeatedly as a scene of prominent action and pious religious practice. Jerusalem is where the rationale for the full inclusion of the Gentiles is hammered out (11.1-18; 15.1-41); it is also where Paul returns to face opposition, as Jesus did before him (21.13) and to make his defense against baseless charges delivered by hostile Jewish opponents (21.17-23.11). Significantly, one way in which Paul defends his piety is to link it with the pious worship of the 'twelve tribes' (26.6-7), thus suggesting that his devotion is quintessentially Israelite.

Authorizing Function of Israelite Scriptures

The speeches of Acts are replete with the citation of scriptures. These citations function in the narrative as proof that the events of which the protagonists speak are nothing less than fulfillment of ancient prophecy. Thus, the phenomenon of speaking in tongues on the day of Pentecost is understood as a fulfillment of the prophet Joel concerning visionary experiences in the last days (2.16-21); the Ethiopian eunuch reads a passage from Isaiah on the suffering righteous, which is demonstrated by Philip to be a prophecy concerning Jesus (8.32-33); the Psalms are cited as proof of Jesus' exalted status (2.34-35; 13.33-35). The final speech of Paul during his captivity in Rome, addressed to Jews in Rome, is a quotation from the prophet Isaiah, which functions to explain Jewish rejection of the gospel as owing to the dullness of their hearts and the blindness of their eyes (28.26-27).

Differently from other canonical Gospel authors, Luke stresses that it is not merely a specific verse of ancient scripture here and there that is fulfilled through the events concerning Jesus and his followers, but rather, it is the scriptures *in their totality* that come to fulfillment in the Christ event. This totalizing view of scriptures is evident both in the Third Gospel (see Lk. 24.44: 'Then Jesus said to them, "These are my words that I spoke to you while I was still with you—*that everything written about me in the law of Moses, the prophets, and the psalms must be fulfilled*"'; my emphasis) and in Acts. For the latter, consider Paul's self-defense while on trial, where he styles himself as someone who has believed '*everything* laid down according to the law or written in the prophets' (24.14; see also 26.22-23).

Relatively Favorable Portrait of Pharisees as Potential Allies of Paul

Among modern dictionary definitions for the word Pharisee, 'hypocrite' is, inevitably, given; in Christian churches, 'Pharisee' is often employed to signify the archetypal villain. Such negative connotations for these religious leaders is a sign of the long-standing influence of the Gospel of Matthew, which has a bone to pick with this group (on the Gospel of Matthew's quarrel with the Pharisees, see especially Matthew 23 and secondary scholarship). If, instead, the two volumes penned by Luke had been the dominant influence on Christian thinking about the Pharisees, Bible dictionaries would read otherwise and sermons would need to come up with another straw figure against which to rail. In Acts, at least some Pharisees are depicted as instruments of good will toward the movement. Early on, the Pharisee, Gamaliel, counsels against the harsh treatment of the apostles, couching his words in shrewd and, perhaps, ironic, advice concerning divine will and the foolishness of trying to flout it (5.33-39). Pharisees are noted among the community of Jesus believers who deliberate concerning the importance of law observance for Gentiles and, presumably, consent with the whole church that such observance should be limited to a few minimal obligations (15.5; cf. 15.22). Twice, in his defense, Paul reminds his listeners that he himself is a Pharisee; he even goes so far as to suggest that the (very Pharisaic) affirmation of the resurrection of the dead lies at the heart of false accusations against him (23.6; 26.5). Pharisaism in Acts, like the Jerusalem Temple and the Jewish scriptures, functions to signify that the movement of Jesus followers is not a new religion that has sprung up from nowhere, but rather is in line with long established institutional practices of Judaism.

Jewish Leadership of the Jesus Movement

Paul's insistence, in the speeches in Acts, that he himself is a Pharisee can also be seen as part of Acts' rhetorical emphasis on not just Jewish institutions, but also the Jewish credentials of the group's leaders (22.3; 23.6; 26.5; cf. Paul's accounts in his own letters which speak of Pharisaism as a part of his 'former' life which he has discarded [Phil. 3.4-8; Gal. 1.13-14]). The Jerusalem apostles are given pride of place among the leadership of the church. Consider, for instance, the choosing of the replacement for Judas (1.12-26) and the constituency of the Jerusalem council (Acts 15.1-29). James, famous among early Christians as the brother of Jesus and the model of Jewish piety (e.g. see the story of James's martyrdom preserved in Eusebius's *Church History* 2.23.4-18), takes part in authorizing the Pauline mission to the Gentiles (15.12-21), greets Paul on his return to Jerusalem at the close of his Gentile ministry and assists Paul in building a defense against charges that he breaks the law (21.17-26). Twice in his own speeches, Paul identifies himself with the emphatic formulation, '*I am a Jew*' (*egō eimi Ioudaios*, 21.39; 22.3). He is depicted as the model of Jewish piety, joining in a rite of purification to deflect charges to the contrary (21.24-26) and asserting that he worships the God of his ancestors, 'believing everything laid down according to the law or written in the prophets' (24.14).

This cursory survey should demonstrate the ways in which the author of Acts does, indeed, embrace things Jewish. This author, then, should be distinguished from the modern anti-Semite who regards all things Jewish with hostility. But the anti-Jewish rub here is not so much *that* he embraces, but *how* he embraces; the operative term here is appropriation. Acts values these aspects of Judaism, but also insists that these Jewish things, when properly understood, point to the messiahship of Jesus. 'True Jews', such as Peter, Paul and James, recognize this. 'True Judaism' is really Christianity in this way of thinking. In this sense, Acts stands in line with the many early Christian authors who wrote treatises against the Jews, and who also insist that the traditions of Israel now belong to them and not to the Jews, who have been disinherited. Hand in hand with this articulation of Christian supersession is the depiction of virtually all Jews who do not confess Jesus as beyond the pale, as we shall see in more detail below.

First, to the Jews

This focus on Jewish institutions and Jewish leadership leads not only to the foregrounding of Jerusalem in the first section of Acts, but also to a particular pattern in Paul's ministry. In Paul's own letters, he describes himself repeatedly as the 'apostle to the Gentiles'. He writes to Gentile audiences and never mentions having spent time in any synagogue during his ministry. In contrast, Acts depicts Paul as perpetually engaged in a two-step ministry: whenever he arrives in a new city, he preaches first in the synagogue and, only after his rejection there, does he turn to approach the Gentiles with his promises.

This is not a subtle patterning on the author's part, but rather something that is made explicit through three direct speeches by Paul on the matter. The first of these speeches, in the synagogue at Pisidian Antioch, expresses the two-step rationale most completely: 'It was necessary that the word of God should be spoken first to you. Since you reject it and judge yourselves to be unworthy of eternal life, we are now turning to the Gentiles' (13.46). The second of these speeches occurs after opposition in the synagogue in Corinth (18.6) and, as already noted above, the third, addressed to Jews in Rome, closes the book (28.28). It should be noted that the rejection of the message by Jews in the synagogue is never said to be total. In each of these three scenes at least some Jews are receptive to the message that Jesus is the messiah.

This receptivity demonstrates Acts' view that at least some Jews understood their own scriptures correctly. (It is also the case that pressing each of Paul's ministry stops into the 'synagogue-first' mold results in at least one implausible, perhaps even comical, scenario: at the close of his second missionary journey, Paul is accompanied by Pricilla and Aquila, who travel with him from Corinth to Syria. But when the ship arrives in Ephesus, he leaves them at the dock while he makes a trip to the synagogue to debate with the Jews there before embarking on the rest of the journey. See 18.18-21.)

The pattern makes sense in view of the question that Gentiles, either within the movement or viewing from the outside, might have had concerning Christians, namely, how could this group assert itself as heirs of the promises to Israel, given its Gentile constituency? How do followers of the Way answer the charge of adhering to a new and false form of piety? The answer provided in this narrative is that the movement *should* have included all Jews and did, indeed, include *some* Jews (the right-thinking Jews). It is now to the Jews, who, from the perspective of the author of Acts, got it all wrong, that we turn.

Beyond the Pale

Good Jews, those faithful pious practitioners like James, Peter, Stephen and Paul, who come to see Jesus as messiah, are the heroes of the story Luke tells in Acts. That 'myriads' of nameless Jews also come to be convinced of Jesus' standing as Christ is celebrated in Acts (21.20). In contrast, most Jews who do not confess Jesus are painted with a dramatically different coloring. The key attributes of those Jews in the narrative who do not confess Jesus are violence and blood lust, aimed first at Jesus during his lifetime and then, subsequently, at his faithful followers.

Peter singles out Judeans, Jerusalemites and/or Israelites more broadly, in six instances within his speeches, as having killed Jesus (2.22-23, 36; 3.12-15a; 4.8b-10a; 5.30; 10.39). Paul suggests that culpability for Jesus' death remains with 'residents of Jerusalem and their leaders' (13.27-28). Stephen levels the accusation of Christ killing against the Jews gathered to hear his defense speech, linking it to the persecution of prophets, which he regards as pervasive among the ancestors (7.51-52). Only once in the narrative is the death of Jesus attributed to the collusion of *both* Jews and Gentiles: 'For in this city, in fact, both Herod and Pontius Pilate, with the Gentiles and the peoples of Israel gathered together against your holy servant Jesus' (4:28–29). (Note also that, in the case where Gentile involvement is acknowledged, the execution of Jesus is described, euphemistically, as a 'gathering together against'. The verb 'to crucify' is used only in cases where Jews are singled out as executioners.)

It is sometimes argued that because, in some of these instances, a spe-cific subgroup is targeted as the Christ killers—either the Jerusalemites or the rulers of the people—Luke does not mean to tar all non-believing Jews with this accusation. But this argument does not account for the instances of the Christ-killing charge which do evoke a more corporate sense of guilt by using designations such as Israelites (2.22; 3.12) or by including Jews from the far corners of the earth among those accused (consider the audi-ence of the Pentecost speech or the audience accused by Stephen). More to the point, it does not account for the fact that, in the Acts' narrative, killing Christ is only one instance of the murderous impulse said to be directed by the Jews against this messianic movement. We now turn to documenting the extent of this murderous impulse, according to Acts.

After Jesus' crucifixion, violent hostility among Jews against followers of the Way continues in Jerusalem, where the council and the high priest are said to wish to kill Peter and all of the apostles (5.27-33). Jews from a vast array of geographical regions are involved in the stoning of Stephen (6.9). Herod's execution of James, the brother of John, is said to be pleasing to 'the Jews' and leads to further expectation that he will kill Peter as well (12.3, 11). The figure of Saul/Paul exemplifies this murderous nature of 'the Jews'. Before his conversion experience, Saul is said to 'breathe threats and murder' (9.1) among Jesus believers; he is also implicated in the death of Stephen (8.1, 3; 22.19-20). But after his conversion, he is on the receiving end of numerous attempts by 'the Jews' to take his life, beginning with a plot to kill him in Damascus (9.23-24); in Lystra, he is actually stoned by Jews, who leave the site of the stoning presuming that they have killed their victim (14.19). This desire to kill Paul drives the action in the closing scenes, where Paul's treat-ment by various state officials is guided by knowledge that Jews would prefer to kill him in cold blood before he can stand trial. Consider 22.22 where the crowd in Jerusalem shouts in one voice for Paul's death after his speech on the Temple steps or the subsequent and elaborate plot with a sacred vow to ambush him while he is in custody in this city (23.12, 14, 21).

These numerous portraits of Jewish violence, aimed at Jesus and then at followers of the Way from Peter and the Apostles, to Stephen and, ulti-mately, to Paul and his traveling companions, make it difficult to argue that Acts is limiting depictions of violent Jews to merely a subgroup of leaders or to a specific narrow location, such as Jerusalem or Judea. Violence may orig-inate in Jerusalem, but 'the Jews' in Jerusalem who are gripped by it come from all corners of the earth. Moreover, the impulse flows outward—from Jerusalem to Caesarea to Lystra to Thessalonica—affecting any geographi-cal region where non-believing Jews encounter followers of the Way.

It is not just that non-believing Jews kill and desire to kill Jesus believers, but the particulars of how that desire is depicted that serve Acts' overall rhetorical strategy to denigrate them in Roman eyes. Elite Romans prided themselves on their legal system, the judiciousness of their trial procedures, their fair, orderly and benevolent treatment of residents in provinces they occupied. What they disdained, in contrast, was mob behavior—extra-legal, impulsive and uncontrolled violence emanating from crowds that threatened to degenerate into *stasis* or rebellion. When non-believing Jews turn on Christians in Acts, it is precisely this sort of mob behavior that they exhibit. The story of the trial and stoning of Stephen provides a good example of how this rhetorical strategy works (Acts 6.8-8.1). At first glance, Stephen seems to be given opportunity for a fair juridical process. He is brought before a council (presumably a formal legal body), interrogated by the high priest and allowed to make a speech in his defense. On closer inspection, however, this juridical process turns out to be a sham, for it degenerates quickly into mob violence. The crowd, hearing his speech, becomes enraged, dragging him out of the city with loud shouts and picking up stones to fling at him. Throwing stones to kill serves in Roman literature to denote a particularly incendiary form of mob behavior and the Stephen pericope is not the only one in which 'the Jews' are said to land upon this means of expressing their violent hostility (cf. Acts 14.5, 19). Moreover, this is not the only form of incendiary behavior in which 'the Jews' are said to engage. Texts describing non-believing Jews' hostility toward believers are littered with language of lawlessness and sedition. Jews stir up mobs (17.5; 21.13), make plots (9.24; 20.3), incite the undesirable elements in the cities (13.50; 14.2), drag innocents from their houses (17.6), deliver false charges (6.13; 17.6; 18.12), shout out chaotically in public settings (7.57; 21.34; 22.22), attempt to kill in cold blood (21.31) and, perhaps most impiously, take solemn oaths to seal their deadly pacts (23.12, 21).

In short, Acts' denigration of Jews operates not on the level of religious customs and institutions, but in the realm of social behavior. It does not criticize Jews for their ritual practices (so long as none among them insists that such practices must be imposed upon Gentiles). It does not call into question the standing of Moses or the prophets and it does not scorn the 'eastern' origins of its religious communities. Instead, it calls into question the civic behavior of the non-believing Jewish community, depicting them just as Tacitus had said they were, from his vantage point after the Jewish War, as a group of imperial subjects 'perpetually engaged in sedition'.

Making Sense of Things

Having demonstrated how Luke's rhetoric functions to appropriate and to denigrate, we now turn to make some qualifying remarks in order to assist readers in sorting through the significance of this anti-Judaism within a corpus of writings deemed sacred by Christians.

First, as noted briefly above, Luke's brand of anti-Judaism is to be distinguished from modern anti-Semitism, insofar as this latter category has been traditionally reserved for racial animus and insofar as race has been traditionally understood as essential and fixed rather than mutable. (It is beyond the scope of this book to elaborate, but let it, at least, be noted here that more recent thinking on the category of race no longer embraces notions of essence or fixity; in the field of early Christianity and race, the work of Denise Buell [2005] is essential.) Acts celebrates Jews—provided that they are right thinking—and, therefore, we are not dealing here with an author who assumes that Jews have a racially inferior essence. The long history of race-based anxiety in the modern West includes much hand-wringing over the question of whether a Jew, owing to her corporeal 'Jewishness', could actually become an authentic Christian convert. In marked distinction, Acts holds a relatively more positive view: Jews who embrace Jesus as Christ are model Christians and their leadership is crucial to the movement's success.

Second, though we may trace the *effect* of rhetorical markers in Acts in denigrating Jews, it is not necessary to insist that the rhetorical effects of this writing prove that Acts' author possessed an unqualifiedly malicious *intent*. It is possible to imagine this author's plight in sympathetic terms. He, undoubtedly, lived in a precarious position, given prejudices that existed against Jews as a social group and against all things suspiciously 'eastern', 'foreign' or strangely new. Writing in the early second century, he would have known of Jesus followers who died at Roman hands, both notable Christians (like Paul and Peter) and also members of churches in Asia Minor, for which Pliny's letter to Trajan concerning Christians serves as one indication. He might also have known of instances in which not only Romans and other 'Gentiles', but also Jews who did not confess faith in Jesus acted violently toward Jesus followers, thus inspiring the violent depictions he constructs.

New Testament scholar, Brigitte Kahl, attempts to capture Luke's precarious plight, in the aftermath of animosities fueled by the Jewish War, from a sympathetic perspective. Noting how he attempts to negotiate between accommodation and resistance, Kahl writes, 'One could view Acts as a voice training, a speech exercise for a narrative whose words had been cut off by the irresistible power of Roman swords. In this regard, Luke's writing is an act of resistant survival in circumstances that rendered any explicit resistance suicidal' (2008: 149).

In view of this plight, we might speak of the anti-Jewish rhetorical markers in the text as an unfortunate by-product of a strategy for defending his own group, rather than the central intent of Luke's undertaking. We could also note that Luke himself, writing from his precarious position under empire, could not have envisioned the full effects that his rhetorical violence would, ultimately, have. Luke's only violent weapon was his words. Only in subsequent iterations of Christian anti-Judaism, once Christianity achieved its privileged place in that empire, did it achieve the power to impose the physical force of the state upon its hated Others.

Finally, it could be acknowledged that the violent rhetorical markers contained in this book of the New Testament might serve to instill a measure of humility in Christians concerning the nature of our scriptures and the manner of their divine inspiration. A commonplace among Christians in certain quarters is that our scriptures communicate solely an ethic of peace and love. Thus, as this line of thinking goes, our scriptures are vastly superior to those of both Jews and Muslims, where violence abounds, from the stories of Joshua's conquest of Jericho to Mohammed's battles in Arabia. Acknowledging that Christian scriptures also contain violent rhetorical markers serving to denigrate Others (alongside messages of peace and love) does the helpful work of deflating such assumptions of superiority. In this way, Christians wishing to engage in interfaith dialogue have their own position complicated and, thus, enriched.

For Further Reading

Brawley, Robert
1987   *Luke-Acts and the Jews: Conflict, Apology and Conciliation* (Atlanta, GA: Scholars Press).
Buell, Denise K.
2005   *Why This New Race: Ethnic Reasoning in Early Christianity* (New York: Columbia University Press).
Kahl, Brigitte
2008   'Acts of the Apostles: Pro(to)-Imperial Script and Hidden Transcript', in *In the Shadow of Empire: Reclaiming the Bible as a History of Faithful Resistance* (ed. Richard Horsley; Louisville, KY: Westminster John Knox Press), pp. 137-56.
Matthews, Shelly
2010   *Perfect Martyr: The Stoning of Stephen and the Construction of Christian Identity* (Oxford: Oxford University Press).
Slingerland, Dixon
1986   '"The Jews" in the Pauline Portion of Acts', *Journal of the American Academy of Religion* 54, pp. 305-21.
Tiede, David
1993   '"Fighting against God": Luke's Interpretation of Jewish Rejection of the Messiah Jesus', in *Anti-Semitism and Early Christianity: Issues of Polemic and Faith* (ed. Craig Evans and Donald Hagner; Minneapolis, MN: Fortress Press), pp. 102-12.
Tyson, Joseph (ed.)
1988   *Luke–Acts and the Jewish People: Eight Critical Perspectives* (Minneapolis, MN: Augsburg).
Wills, Lawrence
1991   'The Depiction of the Jews in Acts', *Journal of Biblical Literature* 110, pp. 631-54.

5

The Pentecost

Aside from the story of Paul's Damascus Road 'conversion', there is no story in Acts better known than the story of the descent of the Holy Spirit on the day of Pentecost. The apostles and other believers, at the command of the risen Lord, remain in Jerusalem, awaiting the next demonstration of divine power. Suddenly, the Spirit descends in a language miracle both visual and aural. Tongues as of fire fall upon the heads of believers, inspiring them to speak in the multiple languages of all the Jews gathered in Jerusalem from every corner of the earth, so that each hears in one's own language. Astonished observers inquire into the meaning of this commotion and, Peter, as chief spokesperson for the group, explains the meaning in an oration so compelling that it results in the conversion of thousands of Jews in Jerusalem.

The text brims with symbolic meaning, primarily in the form of biblical allusion. The speech in multiple languages, which is intelligible to representatives from a myriad of nations, suggests a reversal of the story of the tower of Babel, the confusion of languages in Genesis 11. The rushing wind and fire signal a manifestation of God, a theophany, such as the one before Moses on Mt Sinai. The speech of Peter, explaining the event, builds on multiple citations from the Septuagint. It is as clear in this pericope as in any portion of the book of Acts that the narrative is not a mere transcript of a historical event, faithfully composed to reflect an unmediated reality.

In keeping with our focus on rhetorical reading throughout this guide, this chapter approaches the passage neither as a transcript of a historical event as it really happened nor as a dogmatic statement of Christian teaching concerning the Spirit that cannot be questioned. We approach it, instead, as an argument made by Luke in the midst of a contest and struggle over the meaning of spirit possession in the early community of Jesus believers. Through it, Luke makes a rhetorical assertion concerning the manner by which believers in Jesus became empowered by the Holy Spirit to preach the gospel and the meaning that should be ascribed to that event. As noted above, one obvious source for this composition is the Septuagint, which is both cited explicitly and also alluded to in keeping with the author's concern to demonstrate how unfolding events conform to scriptural prophecy.

But, as is the case with the genre of ancient historiography, this is not to say that Luke operates entirely within the realm of fiction as he composes. He is also working with traditions drawn from historical events concerning a 'spirit movement' among followers of Jesus.

In the pages that follow, I offer a feminist, rhetorical reading of the Pentecost pericope, which includes consideration of the historical phenomenon of this spirit movement among early Jesus followers. It is a rhetorical reading in two senses. First, as noted above, it presumes that the Pentecost narrative is a rhetorical assertion by Luke concerning the meaning, power and work of the Spirit. It works to identify significant rhetorical markers in the text that suggest Luke's own rhetorical tendencies and concerns. It also attempts to read those rhetorical markers against the grain in an effort to capture voices of those with whom Luke struggles. Second, it is a rhetorical reading in the sense that it does not assume to reveal to readers the one true meaning of the passage, but rather attempts to construct a persuasive reading concerning the significance of this text within our contemporary setting. As a feminist historical reading, it has an eye to questions of gender-domination, along with other forms of domination, in the ancient past. It presumes that women and other marginalized persons were actors and agents in the time of emerging Christianity, but that their presence has been diminished, their roles distorted and their voices muted in the kyriarchal, androcentric master narrative of the early Christian movement that was, eventually, accepted as orthodoxy. Thus, it works to recapture those voices and make present their agency in the form of a historical narrative.

Biblical scholars who challenge and critique the historical-critical paradigm are not universally drawn to the project of historical reconstruction. Many feminist, postcolonial and queer exegetes are less interested in historically reconstructed meanings, looking instead to literary or cultural criticism as an entry into the meaning-making process of biblical literature. They might highlight the meanings that ordinary readers have constructed from biblical texts or otherwise identify textual alignments between biblical narratives and contemporary societies. A variety of richly textured readings of biblical texts has been produced from such exegetical approaches, including readings of the Pentecost narrative. (For two such recent readings, see Jobling 2001 and Williams 2009).

In view of the richness of recent literary and cultural readings and the fact that even historical reconstructions that do not operate squarely within the historical-critical paradigm are still influenced by it and employ at least some of its tools, it is necessary to clarify why this chapter opts to do historical reconstruction at all. While the historical-critical method idealizes the pose of neutrality and objectivity and thus of writing history merely for its own sake, it is possible to write history without embracing this framework. The rhetorical-ethical paradigm, in contrast to the historical-critical paradigm, is aligned with new currents in historiography, including feminist historiography and materialist historiography, which understand the process of writing history as an ethical-political exercise, the process of recovering 'dangerous memory'.

Both materialist and feminist historiography hold that historical narratives written by the dominant classes and their scribes are false and falsifying in that they mask the agency of the oppressed and marginalized without whose contributions civilization would not be possible. Engaging in reconstructive projects to reveal these contributions can be, on the one hand, an attempt to redeem the past, a means of enabling present generations to enter into solidarity with all who suffered at what Hegel calls the 'slaughterbench' of history (Benjamin 1969: 256-58). It can also be, on the other hand, politically empowering for the present, a means of inspiring women and other marginalized persons in the present to transform oppressive social relations and unjust political institutions. As Elisabeth Schüssler Fiorenza has noted, in her landmark historical reconstruction project, *In Memory of Her*, 'If the enslavement and colonization of people becomes total when their history is destroyed because solidarity with the faith and suffering of the dead is made impossible, then a feminist biblical hermeneutics has the task of becoming a "dangerous memory" that reclaims the religious suffering and engagement of the dead' (Schüssler Fiorenza 1983: 51). While acknowledging that any author's perspective on how to write such redeeming history is only partial and that my own ability to write transformative historical narrative is certainly limited, it is, nevertheless, in the spirit of such historical projects that the following reading is undertaken.

The 'Orderly Account' of the Spirit's Descent

One of the greatest challenges the author of Acts faced in his attempt to present Theophilus with an orderly account of the early Jesus movement is that a large number of participants in the movement, both in the past generation about whom he writes and also among his contemporaries, understood themselves to be possessed by a divine Spirit.

The ritual performances of one who understands herself to be in a state of divine spirit possession could include the following: speaking ecstatically 'in the tongues of angels', beholding visions, engaging in prophecy in a variety of forms, perceiving oneself to be transported into the heavens, performing wondrous deeds (including exorcisms and other types of healing). Moreover, our sources suggest that members of the early Jesus movement experienced the Spirit as an indiscriminate force, one that was 'no respecter of persons', falling upon both male and female, slave and free, the lowly as well as those of noble birth. From the perspective of an elite outsider, such indiscriminate and ecstatic possession, in which boundaries of all sorts were transgressed and those higher born mixed with the most unseemly elements of society, would appear as anything but orderly.

Given the unwieldy nature of social groups who understand themselves to be in the Spirit's possession, Luke might have preferred to ignore the phenomenon altogether. But this option appears not to have been a viable one, as the presence of the Pentecost story indicates. In the same way that traditions about Roman involvement in the crucifixion of Jesus and the death of Paul were so strong that Luke could not ignore them outright (even though he works to downplay that involvement), so strong also were these traditions of the Spirit's outpouring among believers. Thus, instead of omitting traditions of unwieldy spirit phenomena, Luke works to contain them. This is no easy task, given the subject matter. To borrow a Lukan analogy, the workings of the Spirit were experienced by believers to be as powerful as 'tongues of flame' and fire is no easy element to tame. Luke is able to tell a story of the descent of the Holy Spirit within a reasonably well ordered narrative frame only because he was an exceedingly accomplished and creative author. To be sure, his narrative is *reasonably* well ordered, but not perfectly ordered. We will have opportunity below to examine gaps, fissures and counter narratives within Luke's text—the places where unwieldy traditions concerning spirit phenomena escape the author's controlling hand. But first, we turn to considering rhetorical markers Luke employs in an effort to frame the Spirit's descent in an orderly way.

Fixing the Space and Place

One of the ways Luke works to order the Spirit is to locate its original descent precisely in terms of time and space. The Holy Spirit descends first in Jerusalem, the city of overwhelming importance to Luke's narrative. The Spirit descends on a Holy Day in the Jewish calendar, the day of Pentecost, a pilgrimage festival, which is likely, by the time of Luke's writing, to have been associated with the granting of the Sinai covenant. Further, Luke makes clear that the descent was foreordained as the crucial next step in the advancement of the gospel after the ascension of Jesus; this he does by having Jesus foretell the event in some of the very first words of the book of Acts. According to Acts 1.4, while appearing to the apostles over forty days, Jesus charges them not to leave Jerusalem, but to wait for 'the promise of the Father', namely, baptism by the Holy Spirit.

Privileging the Apostles

It is also clear that Luke wishes to feature the eleven (and eventually, after a replacement for Judas is chosen, the twelve) apostles as somehow being

privileged recipients of the Spirit's power. As noted above, the message concerning the promised descent of the Holy Spirit in the opening chapter of
Acts is not delivered to a large crowd of believers, but, specifically, to the
apostles. While around one hundred and twenty persons are said to constitute this earliest Jerusalem community (1.15) and all of them are said
to become filled with the Holy Spirit on the day of Pentecost (2.4), only
the apostles, along with Mary, the mother of Jesus, are named members of
this incipient community (1.12-14). Finally, for interpretation of the event,
the crowd looks to Peter, who stands, with the eleven other apostles, to
deliver his speech on the meaning of the events that had unfolded. Those
who are baptized upon hearing Peter's explanation of the Spirit miracle,
subsequently bow to apostolic authority ('So those who received [Peter's
preaching] were baptized, and there were added that day about three thousand souls. And they devoted themselves to the apostles' teaching and fellowship', 2.41-42a).

Gendering the Space

In addition to depicting the apostles as having special foreknowledge of the
Spirit's coming and primary authority to interpret its meaning, the story
also conforms to an orderly account in the sense that the exchange concerning the event takes place in an ideally acceptable 'male space'; a public, open-air setting where Peter stands alongside his fellow apostles and
employs oratorical finesse to persuade a group of 'men, brothers' of the truth
of his message. (For a discussion of the highly masculine coding of oratory in
the ancient world and the frequent use of the gender-specific *anēr* in Acts,
see Chapters Two and Three of this guide). Note also that the move, from
the room in which the Spirit descends to the open air in which the event
is interpreted, is sudden and defies verisimilitude; it is difficult to imagine
an open air space, within the residential quarters of the city of Jerusalem,
where a crowd of more than three thousand could gather for such a public
recitation. Finally, while Acts has noted at 1.14a that the group of believers
included women, they have vanished from the narrative at this point.

Making the Unintelligible Plain

Another way that Acts transmits the story of the movement of the Spirit
among believers in a manner that masks the potentially unruly nature of
such possession is to radically foreclose the meaning of spiritual speech.
Glossolalia, speaking in tongues, was a common phenomenon in the ancient
Greco-Roman world. It was an expression of ecstatic speech, unintelligible
to human listeners, but understood to be a form of communion with the

heavenly realm. In the Jewish apocryphal document, *The Testament of Job* (first or second century CE), the daughters of Job are said to possess the gift of ecstatic speech, enabling them to turn away from mere worldly concerns and to sing hymns to God, such as the angels would sing. From documents such as the *Testament of Job* and, also, from Paul's 1 Corinthians, we know that the ability to speak in this unintelligible, angelic language was regarded as a superior gift of the Spirit. (To be sure, Paul attempts to regulate and subordinate such speech in the Corinthian assembly. He exhorts the community there to provide for interpretation of such speech at every gathering and not to allow for such speech unless interpretation can be provided [1 Cor. 14.13-17, 27-28]. But, nevertheless, Paul also makes clear that he understands himself to be in superior possession of this gift, which the Corinthians appear to value so highly. Consider 1 Cor. 14.18: 'I thank God that I speak in tongues more than all of you'.)

Acts sets up the language miracle by explaining that recipients speak in 'other tongues (*heterais glōssais*) given by the Spirit' (2.4), an introduction that, at least, hints at the practice of *glossolalia*. But the speech of those inspired by the Spirit is described by Luke in terms that directly contradict the literal meaning of *glossolalia*. Rather than depicting the speech as unintelligible, Luke depicts it as a form of prophecy that is perfectly clear. Each recipient of a tongue of flame is able to speak in a language that is accessible to listeners of a multitude of nationalities (thus, in 2.8 the crowd asks, 'And how is it that we hear, each of us in his own native language?'). At Acts 2.4, the Greek verb used to describe the gift given by the Spirit is *apophthengomai*, which means to speak one's opinion boldly and plainly (from this verb is derived the English word, apothegm). Thus, Acts asserts that the gift, given to each of the one hundred and twenty believers on the Day of Pentecost, falls closer to the realm of public oratory than ecstatic worship; it is the power to declaim.

To recast *glossolalia* as a form of bold and plain prophetic speech, universally accessible to outsiders, seems to be a direct response to the worry expressed by the apostle Paul in his excursuses on speaking in tongues in the epistle he writes to the Corinthian community. In that epistle, Paul does not prohibit speaking in tongues, but subordinates it to prophecy and admonishes that speaking in tongues should only be practiced within the assembly, if interpretation is also provided. His rationale for limiting speaking in tongues is mission, as 1 Cor. 14.23 indicates ('If the whole church assembles and all speak in tongues, and outsiders or unbelievers enter, will they not say that you are mad?'). Recasting *glossolalia* as prophecy is also consistent with the message, repeated throughout Acts, that official spokespersons for the movement speak openly and with boldness and that anyone with eyes to see and ears to hear could readily understand that message. It is also, on the part of the author of Acts, an astonishingly bold redefinition of what the early Christian experience of speaking in spiritual tongues entailed.

Explaining the Meaning of the Miracle Definitively

A further aspect of the rhetoric of the Pentecost story that moves in the direction of orderliness and security is the fact that outside observers who seek the meaning of the event in which the Spirit descends are given one authoritative answer. Peter, as chief spokesperson for the apostles, produces definitive interpretation by demonstrating, through multiple citations of ancient scriptures, that all that has happened was foretold and should, rightfully, lead to the conversion of the crowd.

The first citation Peter uses as proof that scriptures are being fulfilled in the midst of the crowd is from the prophet Joel, which contains the evocative image of a relatively egalitarian distribution of the Spirit's prophetic gift:

> I will pour out my Spirit upon all flesh,
> and your sons and your daughters shall prophesy,
> and your young men shall see visions,
> and your old men shall dream dreams.
> Even upon my slaves, both men and women,
> in those days I will pour out my Spirit;
> and they shall prophesy.

The significance of this particular citation from Joel to our reading of the Pentecost miracle will merit considerable reflection below. Here it is noted that Peter's 'explanation' of the language miracle devotes little space to the miracle itself. The fact that the group is prophesying prompts the citation of Joel as a means to demonstrate its preordained status and this citation, in turn, is employed as a springboard into a missionary sermon on the need for repentance and conversion to Christ belief. The culminating phrase of the prophetic citation, 'whoever calls on the name of the Lord will be saved', is echoed again, at the end of Peter's exchange with the crowd, when he exhorts them to repent and escape the present generation. But, aside from acknowledging the fact of the prophesying, Peter provides no comment concerning the actual content of the spiritual speech that has been uttered. (From the text preceding Peter's speech, a reader gleans the indirect information that those who are inspired by the tongues of flame are 'telling the mighty works of God' [2.11].) Once Peter refutes the accusation that the speakers are drunk and accounts for their speech through citation of the prophets, there is no further reference to the presence of the believers speaking these prophecies; they have no further agency in the text.

Verses 22-36 shift from the language miracle to an expanded proof that
Jesus is God's promised messiah, a core statement of Lukan Christology,
involving detailed exegesis of Psalms, a common practice in messianic
debates by early Christians. In this central section of the speech, the gift
of the Spirit receives only a passing reference (v. 33). In short, after the
citation from Joel concerning the egalitarian distribution of the Spirit's
gift, Peter seems almost to change the subject, turning from the somewhat
unwieldy language miracle to a traditional Christian missionary speech concerning the proclamation of Jesus as messiah, the guilt of 'the Jews' for his
death, the vindication of Jesus through the resurrection and the possibility
of salvation open to all, dependent on the need for repentance and conversion to belief in Jesus as messiah.

Peter's definitive interpretation of the Spirit's work among the crowd
is also remarkable in that no hint is given of a dissenting point of view
concerning spirit phenomena among the early Jesus believers. In thinking
here about the way Luke has treated his source material, it is instructive to
compare the issue of speaking in tongues and spiritual gifts with the issue of
circumcision and dietary laws.

On the one hand, we know from the Pauline epistles, especially Galatians
and Romans, that the question of how extensively the lives of Gentile Jesus
believers should be governed by the Torah was a critical point of dissention
among early believers. Acts acknowledges these debates and gives them
a central place in its narrative: in Acts 10 (concerning the conversion of
Cornelius), Acts 11 (Peter's justification of his practice of eating with the
'uncircumcised') and Acts 15 (the council at Jerusalem).

On the other hand, we also know, from Paul's letter to the Corinthians,
that no small amount of dissension had been generated in Corinth concerning the meaning of spirit phenomena, including the practice of *glossolalia*,
and the boundaries of women's authority to pray and prophesy in the assembly. Based on the defensive tone he adopts repeatedly in the Corinthian
correspondence, Paul's own authority to prescribe the boundaries of spiritual practice appears also to be a disputed question. But, in the matter of
dissenting traditions concerning the meaning of spiritual gifts, Acts treats
its source material quite differently. Disputes concerning the meaning of
spirit phenomena among early believers play no role in the Pentecost narrative. The right of women to pray or prophesy within the assembly is never
disputed, but only because the question is never raised. The worry concerning the unintelligibility of tongues is also not raised, and need not be
raised, given the fact that the Spirit descending on Pentecost gives the gift
of clear speech. In short, Acts' rhetorical strategy concerning circumcision
and dietary laws is to acknowledge initial dissension, but then, in a series
of lengthy pericopes, to suggest that dissension gives way to harmonious

agreement. In contrast, Acts' rhetorical strategy concerning spirit phenomena is to remain silent on the controversy altogether.

It should also be noted that a pattern that has received much attention in previous chapters is woven starkly into the content of this speech. Among the many ways that Peter's one speech imposes an 'orderly' meaning on the Pentecost event is to underscore Jewish agency for the crucifixion. Peter's speech functions to redirect the concerns of readers who might wonder whether those who revere a man subjected to the punishment reserved for the most degraded subjects of empire might also harbor hostile feelings toward the Roman state. Blame for the execution, which has, ultimately, resulted in the Pentecost miracle, is bluntly directed at the Jewish audience to whom he speaks. Peter notes that Jesus is the one whom '*you* nailed and killed by the hands of the lawless' (2.23; my emphasis). Indeed, the last word of Peter, before the audience is brought to repentance, is the second blunt reminder that not the Romans, but the audience to whom he speaks, is the 'you' who crucified Jesus (2.36).

Containing the Egalitarian Impulse of the Spirit within Acts 2

One final way that Acts diffuses the impact of traditions of an unruly Spirit movement among Jesus believers is to evoke the phenomenon in Acts 2, but then to remain aloof from the phenomenon for the remaining twenty-six chapters of the book. As noted above, the quotation from Joel in Acts 2 suggests that the language miracle has involved the descent of the Spirit upon both men and women, young and old, male slaves and female slaves.

But, though a reader might anticipate that this citation from the prophet Joel, in the first speech in Acts, serves as programmatic for the rest of the narrative, it does not. At two further points in the narrative, Acts makes passing reference to *glossolalia* in association with communal baptism (10.46; 19.6), but the phenomenon is never again a point of focus in the narrative. There are no instances, in the chapters that follow, of male slaves and female slaves prophesying or speaking in tongues, though they are part of the believing communities. The only slave, in the subsequent narrative, who delivers a prophecy is not working on behalf of the God of Israel, but rather the god, Apollo (indicated by the reference to her 'Pythian spirit', which is associated with the oracle of Apollo in Delphi [16.16]). Furthermore, she is not portrayed sympathetically. A hint that women within the community of believers possess the gift of prophecy is given in a reference to the four prophesying daughters of Philip in Acts 21.9. But this reference is only given in passing, they are not depicted in speaking roles and Acts remains silent on the content and significance of their prophecy. Subsequent speaking roles for prophetic figures in the book of Acts, along with subsequent recipients of visionary experiences, are limited only to one category of persons marked out by Joel: the young men—*neaniskoi*—especially Peter, Stephen and Paul.

Reading against the Grain

We have identified above rhetorical strategies employed by the author of Acts both to acknowledge the presence of the Spirit within the early Christian community and to contain that Spirit within his orderly prose narrative. Our task now is to read those markers against the grain, identify places of rupture within that orderly narrative and pay attention to counter narratives that might be perceived if one resists the rhetorical markers of the text. Through this resistant reading, our aim is to evoke additional stories about spirit phenomena among believers beyond those that Luke allows.

We are aided in resisting Luke's rhetorical markers and, thus, in unraveling the narrative he presents, by the subject matter before us. As noted above, Luke attempts to tell a story of the orderly descent of the Spirit, but such a phenomenon is not particularly conducive to order. Because Luke is 'playing with fire' here, we can identify places where the flames have escaped the boundaries he has erected in his attempt to contain it. We turn now to identifying places in the text where the narrative loses its coherence, where counter narratives appear to unsettle Luke's concern for order, where alternate voices seem to be pushing through the fabric of the text. To be sure, these places will not be seized upon as reflecting actual historical events in any simple way. But we will gather these passages up as indications that Luke knows other stories that could be told of spirit possession among Jesus believers.

Loose Ends

The many ways in which Luke's story defies verisimilitude provide one hint that Luke is dealing with a much bigger phenomenon than he can control in his narrative. We have already made mention of the impossibility of securing an open-air space in the residential section of Jerusalem in which a gathering of more than three thousand persons could be accommodated. The crowd's ability to observe and absorb the language miracle itself is also difficult to imagine. The hundred and twenty believers are in a large house (as such a house would be needed to accommodate so many) when the Spirit descends. The crowd of diaspora Jews is, apparently, drawn to gather outside of the house at the sound of the commotion and can, apparently, ascertain that those inside are Galilean. One might wonder whether there is some visual indication that the house is occupied by Galileans or whether it is the case that, when they hear 'in their own language', each listener ascertains that their language is being spoken in a Galilean accent. But further, how does the Cretan, for instance, ascertain not only that a recitation of the mighty works of God is taking place in the language spoken on the island of Crete, but also ascertain that the Phrygians, Pamphylians, Parthians, Egyptians, etc. are hearing these things in their tongues as well?

If conventions of verisimilitude were of concern, there would need to be acknowledgement of some form of conferencing among hearers of the languages where the experiences were confirmed. And then there are questions concerning how much explanation Peter's speech really provides. Even the very first citation from Joel raises more problems than solutions. To name but one, the prophet does not speak of a miracle involving translation into multiple languages. In short, the untidy nature of the story—the abrupt shifts, the loose ends, the sequence of unlikely scenarios—suggests that the author has come to a place in his story where the threads cannot be tightly woven.

Points of Tension

Some of the vivid and dramatic details of the narrative also stand in tension with rhetorical markers that point in the direction of order, clarity and security. For one, the initial depiction of the Spirit's descent hints at the frightening and, potentially, uncontrollable power that early believers experienced in the form of spirit possession. As Richard Pervo translates 2.2-3, 'A sudden noise from above, like the roar of a strong rushing wind, filled the house in which they were sitting. Phenomena resembling jagged fiery tongues appeared. One of these settled upon each person' (2009: 58). While the subsequent narrative interprets this image within orderly male space and supplies Peter's reassuring oratory concerning its meaning, readers who pause at this point in the narrative to contemplate the image evoked with these words—roaring wind, flames, a myriad of ragged tongues, more than one hundred people speaking different languages simultaneously—might be more startled than reassured. Through use of these images, Luke himself paints a portrait of a powerfully unsettling phenomenon within the midst of the believing community, even as he attempts to tame it.

Dissenting Voices

It is also the case that the split reaction of the crowd to the language miracle gives us a hint of the unsettling nature of spiritual speech, even if Luke frames that speech as bold and intelligible prophecy. While a portion of the crowd marvels that they have each heard in their own language, dissenters in the crowd mock with accusations of drunkenness (2.13). Drunkenness was a common slur against ecstatic prophets in the ancient world by those who derided them. That Luke allows the dissenting view that those who speak must be 'drunk' hints at a wider range of interpretation of the behavior of those who understood themselves to have been inspired by the Spirit than is offered through Peter's speech.

The Role Not Assigned to the Apostles

Furthermore, however much Luke gives preference to the Twelve by underscoring their privileged foreknowledge and their authority to interpret the significance of the Spirit's descent, he does not (and, perhaps, he dares not?) tell a story in which the Pentecost Spirit itself is *mediated* by the apostles. The Twelve play no role in the actual descent of the Spirit and the Spirit falls directly and expansively upon *all* the believers gathered together ('[*T]hey were all together* in one place ... there appeared to them tongues as of fire, *distributed and resting on each one of them. And they were all filled* with the Holy Spirit', Acts 2.1-4; my emphasis). Acts does not name those upon whom the Spirit falls and they fade from view as Peter speaks. But readers who focus on the description of the descent of the Spirit itself, rather than on the framing details in which the apostles are privileged, ascertain that the Spirit blows where it will and that the apostles have no authority to decide upon whom it should land and what gifts it should instill. (Such a view of the Spirit's indiscriminate descent is not held by the author of the Pastoral Epistles, who views spiritual gifts as transmitted through institutional hierarchy. Thus, the 'gift' given to Timothy is described as one he received 'through prophecy with the laying on of hands by the council of elders' [1 Tim. 4.12].)

Joel's Prophetic Vision

If we needed to settle upon only one of the Pentecost story's details as the point at which Luke has let the cat out of the bag—that is, where the author has revealed what he was attempting to conceal and where a reader who resists the story of the Spirit's descent as a hegemonizing, orderly affair might get a toe hold—it would be the fact that Acts chooses Joel 3.1-5 as the first scriptural citation with which to explain the Pentecost event. The egalitarian vision central to the citation bears repeating: 'This was what was spoken by the prophet Joel: "I will pour out my Spirit on all flesh, and your sons and your daughters shall prophesy and your young men shall see visions and your old men shall dream dreams; indeed on my male slaves and my female slaves in those days I will pour out my Spirit; and they shall prophesy'" (2.16-18, my translation).

The choice of this passage to explain the Spirit's outpouring startles for a number of reasons, many of them tied to the androcentric and kyriarchal concerns of the Acts narrative highlighted above. The choice of twelve male authorities to preside over the believing community had been previously underscored; the women, save for passing reference to Mary, the mother of Jesus, are cloaked in anonymity; the open air setting for Peter's speech on the meaning of the event signals the deliberation of free elite men of the city; the (elite) maleness of the addressees is foregrounded in the pericope. But in this first scriptural citation, Luke betrays, or reveals, a breach in the elite, hyper-masculine edifice he is attempting to construct. Readers are reminded of the Spirit's indiscriminate descent and of the many kinds of persons who adhere to the movement and who practice charismatic gifts. (The citation from Joel, remarkably, mirrors the critical assessment of the composition of early Christian communities offered by the Roman governor, Pliny, in his famous letter to the emperor, Trajan. Writing in the province of Bithynia in Asia Minor in 110 CE, Pliny notes that the movement he scorns as a superstition is composed of persons from 'every age, every rank and also of both sexes', with female slaves as its ministers [Pliny, *Ep.* 10.96]).

Sterner authorities in the emerging Christian movement will not choose to reflect upon this egalitarian vision from Joel (it is impossible to imagine, for instance, the author of the Pastoral Epistles, with his concern to silence women and subordinate slaves, conceding that such a prophecy had been fulfilled within the believing community). A myriad of scriptural citations could have been chosen by Luke as a means of proving that a group of Jesus believers, filled with the spirit and telling of the mighty works of God, fulfilled ancient prophecy. Luke's choice of this particular vision suggests that he knows of such an egalitarian current among Jesus believers. How he arrives at this passage as the primary lens for interpreting the Pentecost event cannot be fully explained. But it seems not unreasonable to imagine that he draws on this pericope because it has been central to early Christian self-understanding in some quarters, even though he has neglected to consider how this choice conflicts with his overarching rhetorical aim to frame the movement in orderly, kyriocentric terms.

Other Readings of the Pentecost

Before engaging in a historical reconstruction, we first consider, briefly, how subsequent readers have received and responded to this narrative of the Spirit's descent among early Jesus believers. From this consideration, we can judge Luke's attempt to frame the story of spirit phenomena among early believers in an orderly and secure manner as largely, but not perfectly, successful.

On the one hand, the orthodox, kyriarchal Christian tradition, which emerged and consolidated its power in centuries subsequent to the composition of Acts, has read the story largely as Luke would have them read it. This is easily observable especially in terms of the way Luke's claims for apostolic privilege and leadership in interpreting the movement of the Holy Spirit have been embraced and expanded by kyriarchal leadership structures in Christian churches throughout the centuries. To cite one ready example of such embrace, the argument against the ordination of women in the Catholic church in the twenty-first century is still framed as the necessary outcome of Jesus' choice of twelve *male* apostles as his earthly representatives (even though maleness, as an explicit and necessary criterion for apostleship, is first articulated only by Peter in Acts 1 and the tradition of 'the Twelve' is not uniformly established across the canonical Gospel traditions). Many Protestant churches, even if they are less hierarchically organized, still point to the privileged place of the apostles in the story and the fact that those inspired by the spirit are not privileged in the same way as justification for their own exclusion of women from leadership roles in their churches.

Moreover, Luke's emphasis on the Spirit's inspiration as the gift of rational speech has been compatible with hegemonic forms of Christianity that have deemphasized and discouraged (when they have not forbidden outright) discourse about, and performance of, spirit possession. This 'more rational' understanding of spirit possession as enlightened speech, to which the educated male elite have special access, has also been widely influential among biblical scholars. Biblical scholars will occasionally frame the issue of early Christian rituals of spirit possession favorably; some consider the likelihood that they involved trance states, shamanistic ritual performance and egalitarian social practices as would have been common among religious groups viewed as 'deviant' by the majority culture (e.g. see Smith 1978; Mount 2005; Mount 2010; and Wire 1990 [a study of the Corinthians which is highly sympathetic to the spiritual experiences of those with whom Paul argues]). Yet, when majority scholarship considers what spiritual possession could have meant for Jesus believers, it has generally assumed a model of inspiration more like the one constructed by Luke—that is, one closer to the realm of oratory than ecstatic worship. In short, Luke's containment of the story of a wide outpouring of the Spirit to the second chapter of Acts and his subsequent narrative of elite male apostles taking charge has been the road taken by large swaths of the Christian church throughout the centuries.

But other roads have also been taken, confirming that alternate reading communities have resisted Acts' hegemonizing frame. Though the egalitarian prophecy from Joel does not become central to early Christian self-understanding in every quarter, we do have one text, from the early third century, which frames an important story of life, death and early Christian meaning-making with this egalitarian prophecy of the last days. The story of the martyrdom of two Christian heroines, the highborn Perpetua and her female slave, Felicity, is a highly marked text in terms of gender and class. The conflict for both women centers around issues of childbearing—Perpetua has a nursing infant she must leave behind on the road to martyrdom and Felicity is pregnant, providentially delivering just before she joins her mistress in the arena. Perpetua engages in conflict with her high-born father and Felicity's status as slave is also underscored. This story of Christian martyrs, which challenges dominant powers through exaggerated focus on heroines whose agency defies class and gender constraints, is prefaced with the citation from Joel as a means to justify continuing inspiration of the Spirit (*Pass. Perp.* 1.4).

Turning to an example of an expansive reading of the Pentecost narrative from the more recent past, one might consider the importance of the Pentecost narrative in the African American ecclesial tradition. As Demetrius Williams has recently documented, a number of African American women called to preaching ministries in the late nineteenth and twentieth century, including Jarena Lee and Julia A. Foote, justified their calling through a democratizing reading of Acts 2. The Azuza Street revival of 1906–1909, instigated by the African-American traveling preacher W.J. Seymour, brought together persons of diverse racial backgrounds— including Blacks, Mexicans, Asians and Anglo-Americans—to participate in ecstatic worship. Women preachers and exhorters were also welcomed by Seymour into the movement. The interracial worship, involving women as well as men, was understood as a miraculous manifestation of the Pentecost prophecy of Joel. The broad participation of Whites with those of other races in the Azuza Street movement was only temporary and Seymour's initial openness toward women did not translate into the acceptance of ordained women in the Church of God in Christ (COGIC), the black denomination that had its roots in this revival. But the early democratic impulses of the movement found inspiration in the reading of the Pentecost pericope in Acts (Williams 2009).

The potential of the Pentecost pericope to inspire liberating readings is also evident in the fact that biblical scholars cite the diversity of languages produced by the Spirit as a means to invoke a burgeoning variety of approaches to biblical interpretation, especially approaches of traditionally marginalized communities (Segovia 1995; Bailey, Liew, Segovia, 2009). Furthermore, in his postmodern reading of the Pentecost pericope, David Jobling considers two quite disparate instances in which the Pentecost story has recently been read in a democratizing direction (Jobling 2001). The first is by the theorist Michel Serres, who extols the Pentecost event as a system of communication instigated by the Spirit in which 'interpretations flow simultaneously in all directions' without an 'externally imposed authorizing system' (Jobling 2001: 214). The second is by participants in a Bible study, sponsored by the World Council of Churches, composed of representatives from aboriginal and formerly colonized peoples, who use the Pentecost story as a springboard to reflect on the fundamental problem of vernacular languages versus common language in situations where the common language is that of the colonizers.

These examples of democratizing readings of the Pentecost pericope signal efforts to cut against the grain of the order Luke attempts to impose. Luke may have attempted to contain the egalitarian spirit movement within the second chapter of his narrative, but the images of the Spirit's descent in wind and flame have been too powerful to be so contained. The wide circle of those invoked as recipients of, and witnesses to, the Spirit's power continue to inspire arguments for inclusiveness, justice and equality. We turn now, finally, to imagining more fully those strands of the early Christian movement that, inspired by the force of a democratizing Spirit, also struggled for inclusiveness, justice and equality.

Imagining What Luke Attempts to Suppress

I have argued that, in the Pentecost narrative, Luke reveals more than he intends; he preserves in the text signs of a spirit movement among early Christian believers which is more unwieldy and has a stronger egalitarian impulse than he would prefer to emphasize for the benefit of Theophilus. The images of rushing wind and flame evoke most clearly the movement's potentially disruptive power; the wide diversity of languages and the expansive citation from the prophet Joel reveal most clearly its democratizing tendencies.

It is possible to expand on a reconstruction of the historical nature of this movement by reading Acts 2 against other ancient texts that provide alternate perspectives on events in the early church. In this case, we have numerous texts upon which we might draw because of the many textual indications of spiritual phenomena among early Jesus believers both from the first generation of Jesus believers and also from the time in which Luke writes. A larger project would consider spirit phenomena within Jesus traditions as preserved in the canonical Gospels, within developing traditions concerning Mary Magdalene, along with the focus on divine spirit in so-called gnostic traditions, within the 'New Prophecy' movement in Phrygia (referred to as Montanism in heresiological tradition) among others.

Limits of space require us to focus here on the Pauline epistles, especially 1 Corinthians, but addressing the question of egalitarian impulses in the Pauline churches best begins with consideration of Gal. 3.28.

Galatians 3.28 within Pauline Tradition

Galatians 3.28 has long been the *locus classicus* for those arguing that early Jesus believers were part of a movement with egalitarian impulses. Together with its preface in v. 27, the passage reads: 'As many of you as were baptized into Christ have clothed yourselves with Christ. There is no longer Jew or Greek, there is no longer slave or free, there is no longer male and female; for all of you are one in Christ Jesus.' It is widely acknowledged among biblical scholars that 3.28 is not an original insight of the apostle Paul, but that here Paul makes reference to an earlier (and, thus, *pre-Pauline*) liturgical formula uttered as part of the ritual of baptism of believers into the Jesus-following group. For Paul himself, the formula matters especially because of the Jew–Gentile pairing, for this pairing is crucial to his arguments concerning the standing of Gentiles within the community of believers in the Galatian assembly. Early feminist exegesis of the passage focused especially on the third pairing of the formula—no male and female—arguing that this pre-Pauline baptismal formula proclaimed the absolving of gender hierarchies and patriarchal marriage. Those with concern for slavery and class issues noted also the apparent nullification of slave status in the formula as well.

Subsequent scholarly commentary on the passage has been voluminous and much of it has been aimed in the direction of curbing what has been regarded as 'excess feminist enthusiasm' in interpretations arguing that the formula had egalitarian social consequences for believers in the first century. Much of this subsequent commentary insists that arguments for an ancient utopia with regards to gender, class and ethnicity are inevitably anachronizing. Many scholars attempting to curb this feminist enthusiasm have focused on the writings of Paul himself, noting that his own authoritarian, kyriocentric impulses spread throughout his correspondence; this, as the argument goes, indicates that Paul was not a gender egalitarian, in spite of what Gal. 3.28 might suggest (e.g. see Martin 2006). It has been noted further that, because ancient Greco-Roman ideology privileged masculinity as vastly superior to femininity, any pronouncement abolishing difference between male and female could imagine that abolition only in terms of females 'becoming male'. Others have noted that the pervasiveness of slavery as an institution in the early centuries of the common era and the, apparently, widespread acceptance of the institution among Jesus believers casts serious doubt over any argument for an egalitarian edge to the formula concerning slaves.

I myself am persuaded by arguments that Gal. 3.28 preserves signs of a struggle among some adherents of the Jesus movement to realize a democratic utopian society, with the following caveats: first, with Mary Ann Beavis, I hold that utopian movements with democratic tendencies, both ancient and modern, are best understood on a sliding scale (as opposed to, say, perfectly embodied democracies). No matter how much a utopian vision gestures toward equality, its embodiment in society can always only be partial owing to the kyriarchal limitations of the culture in which it is practiced. Therefore, I understand Gal. 3.28 as an ideal that some Jesus believers aimed to embody within community, even if it was not realized fully. (Thus, for instance, even if it is conceded that in the ancient Greco-Roman imaginary the proclamation 'no male and female' could only be conceived in terms of females 'becoming male', this is still a more democratic option than disallowing the possibility that females could achieve this 'superior' human status.) Second, I do not regard the dominant voices within canonical texts—in this case the voice of 'Paul himself' or the voice of 'Luke himself'—as the measure of whether such egalitarian impulses were present in early assemblies (*ekklēsiai*). It is, rather, reading against these dominant voices that traces of this movement can be glimpsed.

Thus, I side with those who argue that the pre-Pauline formula preserved in Gal. 3.28 serves as indication that, within the geographic regions Paul traverses and that Luke, subsequently, charts in Acts, baptism into the Spirit of the Lord Jesus was understood by a number of believers as a social leveling phenomenon. Indeed, the pre-Pauline baptismal formula and a pervasive understanding of it in democratizing terms, might serve as explanation for the turn to the prophecy from Joel 2.28-29 as a means of understanding early Christian prophetic practice, since the two texts mirror each other in their democratizing force.

Though biblical scholar, Christopher Mount, approaches the Pauline text without asserting any alliance between his own work and that of feminist biblical interpretation, he has recently proposed an understanding of experience of spirit possession by early Jesus believers that conforms to the reconstruction proposed here. Mount imagines the democratized perception of those possessed by the spirit of Jesus in even more expansive terms, arguing that it included also the collapse of barriers between mortals and gods. His words are worth quoting in full:

> Those possessed by the spirit of Jesus in these early Christ-cults declared 'ABBA', in a ritual apotheosis that collapsed the separation between mortals and gods (Rom. 8.12-39; Gal. 4.1-7). With the confession *Kyrios Iēsous* [Lord Jesus] these communities imagined the cosmic defeat of death and a new social order in which the identity of one possessed by the spirit of Jesus

was no longer determined by social dichotomies that defined physical bodies in the Roman Empire: Jew-Gentile, free-slave, male-female [...]. In short, the communal utterance *Kyrios Iēsous* constructed a discourse about spirit possession that sustained the plausibility of belief in a salvation from cosmic and social forces of oppression felt by at least some, if not many, inhabitants of the early Roman Empire (Mount 2010: 324).

First Corinthians as a Guide to a Democratized Reading of Acts 2

Though it is in Galatians that the pre-Pauline baptismal formula is preserved in fullest form, the Corinthian correspondence provides a more expansive indication of the democratizing force of this early Christian spirit movement. It is in 1 Corinthians that we catch glimpses of the cacophony of a worshiping community in which many participants practice *glossolalia* (1 Cor. 14); in which *all* are characterized by Paul as having been 'enriched in speech and knowledge of every kind', so that they do not lack any spiritual gift (1.4,7); in which slaves are exhorted to seize any opportunity for freedom (7.21); in which both slave and free are proclaimed to have been baptized into one body and to drink of the same spirit (12.13); in which women pray and prophesy within the community and insist, against all cultural pressures to the contrary, that they are right to do so with their heads uncovered (11.2-16).

The evocative scholarship of Antoinette Wire has helped us to imagine, especially, the Corinthian women prophets and their experience of baptism into the Lord Jesus (1990). She argues that these women within the Christ believing community understood themselves as persons rich in God's wisdom, embodying the image and glory of God and speaking with authority. Indeed, we might imagine them as having first turned to the prophet Joel in their searching of the scriptures to explain their own exalted status as prophets of God in the last days. Of course, the line of transmission, from earliest Jesus believing communities reflecting upon Joel 2 as a means of understanding their experience of the democratizing force of the Spirit to Luke's eventual incorporation of that scripture into his Pentecost narrative, is lost to us. But imaging the prophetic community in Corinth as one place where such reflections on the vision of Joel took place is plausible, given what we know of the democratizing impulses of the Jesus believing assemblies in that city.

For Further Reading

Bailey, Randall C., Tat-siong Benny Liew and Fernando F. Segovia (eds.)
2009   *They Were All Together in One Place? Toward Minority Biblical Criticism* (Atlanta, GA: Society of Biblical Literature).

Beavis, Mary Ann
2007   'Christian Origins, Egalitarianism and Utopia', *Journal of Feminist Studies in Religion* 23, pp. 27-49.
Benjamin, Walter
1969   *Illuminations: Essays and Reflections* (trans. Harry Zohn; ed. Hannah Arendt; New York: Schocken Books).
Jobling, David
2001   'Postmodern Pentecost: A Reading of Acts 2', in *Postmodern Interpretations of the Bible: A Reader* (ed. A.K.A. Adam; St Louis, MO: Chalice), pp. 207-17.
Martin, Dale
2006   'The Queer History of Galatians 3.28', in *Sex and the Single Savior: Gender and Sexuality in Biblical Interpretation* (Louisville and London: Westminster John Knox Press), pp. 77-90.
Mount, Christopher
2005   '1 Corinthians 11:3-16: Spirit Possession and Authority in a Non-Pauline Interpolation', *Journal of Biblical Literature* 123, pp. 313-40.
2010   'Religious Experience, the Religion of Paul, and Women in Pauline Churches', in *Women and Gender in Ancient Religions* (ed. Stephen P. Ahearne-Kroll et al.; Tübigen: Mohr Siebeck), pp. 323-47.
Pervo, Richard
2009   *Acts: A Commentary* (Hermeneia; Minneapolis, MN: Fortress Press).
Schüssler Fiorenza, Elisabeth
1983   *In Memory of Her: A Feminist Theological Reconstruction of Christian Origins* (New York: Crossroad).
Segovia, Fernando, F.
1995   '"And They Began to Speak in Other Tongues": Competing Modes of Discourse in Contemporary Biblical Criticism', in *Reading from This Place. I. Social Location and Biblical Interpretation in the United States* (ed. Fernando F. Segovia and Mary Ann Tolbert; Minneapolis, MN: Fortress Press), pp. 1-32.
Smith, Morton
1978   *Jesus the Magician: Charlatan or Son of God?* (San Francisco: Harper & Row).
Williams, Demetrius
2009   '"Upon All Flesh": Acts 2, African Americans, and Intersectional Realities', in Bailey, Liew and Segovia (2009), pp. 289-310.
Wire, Antoinette Clark
1990   *The Corinthian Women Prophets: A Reconstruction through Paul's Rhetoric* (Minneapolis, MN: Fortress Press).

INDEX OF AUTHORS

Acts

INDEX OF SUBJECTS